JAMES JOYCE

David Pritchard

GEDDES & GROSSET

This edition published 2001 by Geddes & Grosset, an
imprint of Children's Leisure Products Limited

© 2001 Children's Leisure Products Limited, David Dale
House, New Lanark ML11 9DJ, Scotland

ISBN 1 84205 049 4

Printed and bound in Scotland

CONTENTS

CHAPTER I

THE EARLY YEARS

James Joyce was not a man to underestimate his own importance, and if asked what great event took place in 1882 he might well have replied that he was born in that year. Yet 1882 was notable in Irish history for a number of other reasons. Politically speaking its most consequential event was the signing of the 'Kilmainham Treaty' between Charles Stewart Parnell, leader of the Irish Home Rule Party, and the English Prime Minister William Ewart Gladstone. The deal resulted in a series of land reforms that changed the face of rural Ireland and in time broke up the great estates of the Anglo-Irish ascendancy. Political unrest in Ireland that year resulted in two notable terrorist attacks – the Phoenix Park murders of Lord Lieutenant Cavendish and Secretary Burke, and the Maamtrasna massacre of a family of five peasants on the present borders of Counties Mayo and Galway. The second crime was followed by the conviction and hanging of three men, and the imprisonment of several others. By the purest of coincidences most of those involved in the mass murder – victims, perpetrators and witnesses – bore the surname Joyce.

The descendants of the Joyce clan are widely scattered throughout Ireland, where it is a common surname. Anglo-

Norman in origin, it is believed to derive from the French *joyeux*, 'joyous'. The Joyces of Connaught, listed as one of the 'twelve tribes' of Galway city, were associated with the mountainous area north of Connemara, which even today is still called the 'Joyce's country'. John Joyce, the father of the famous writer, claimed descent from the Galway Joyces, although he had no evidence to back up his belief. For as far back as could be traced his forebears had lived in Cork; as likely as not they belonged to a totally separate branch of the family. In the early nineteenth century the great-grandfather of the writer was a small-time trader in the rural hinterland of the city of Cork. But in 1848, with the marriage of his son James to Ellen O'Connell, a member of one of Cork's most prosperous merchant dynasties, his family's fortunes improved rapidly. The following year saw the birth of the couple's only child, a son named John Stanislaus Joyce.

John Stanislaus Joyce's father died at the early age of thirty-nine in 1866, leaving a substantial estate to his wife and son. The youthful John Joyce was quick-tongued, garrulous and a natural athlete, but he soon showed himself to be inept and reckless with money. At Queen's College Cork, where he studied medicine between 1867 and 1870, he excelled at athletics and amateur dramatics, but displayed little aptitude for his studies. On his twenty-first birthday he came into his inheritance, which gave him an income of £300 per annum from properties in Cork; at the same time he received the gift of a £1,000 from his grandfather. Joyce left the College before completing his degree, and by 1874 was living in Dublin, where he lost £500 after buying a share in a distillery that went broke. He joined the United Liberal Club, and in 1880 was rewarded for his efforts on their behalf with a well-paid position in the office of the Collector of Rates for Dublin. Shortly afterwards John Joyce proposed to Mary Jane Murray, a young woman he had met in the choir at the Church of the Three Patrons in Rathgar.

Mary Jane Murray, or May as she was usually known, was only twenty years old at the time of her wedding to the dashing Cork man. Her father, John Murray, was the owner of a wine and spirit merchants in Dublin's Clanbrassil Street, but the family's origins were in Longford. Mary Jane, a pretty blonde girl, was quiet and self-composed, a strong contrast to her sociable and outgoing future husband. The Murrays prided themselves on their musical talents, and their daughter had studied at the Misses Flynn's – a house on Usher's Island where two of her maternal aunts taught singing and the piano. Since John Joyce was also a fine singer the couple seemed well suited to each other, but the proposed marriage met strong opposition from their parents. John Murray had heard reports that his future son-in-law was a heavy drinker and well known amongst his friends as a ruthless womanizer. He thought the match would be a disaster for his gentle and pliable daughter, and only let the marriage go ahead after May begged her mother to intercede with him. John's mother Ellen, on the other hand, considered the plebeian Murray family to be socially inferior to her son's O'Connell relations, and would have nothing to do with them. She refused to give her blessing to the union, and returned to Cork before the wedding ceremony. The mother and son never made up their differences, and remained estranged until her death shortly afterwards. The simmering feud between the Cork man and John Murray, whom he usually called 'the old fornicator' because he had been married twice, festered for years, and was extended to include May's brothers William and John (Red).

The Murrays played a prominent role in the childhood of James Joyce, and are recalled in his stories and novels. William and Red Murray are Alphy and Joe in the *Dubliners* story 'Clay', whilst in *Ulysses* William is Richie Goulding and Red appears under his own name. In the story 'Counterparts' he used an incident witnessed by his brother Stanislaus, who heard William's son beg his drunken father: 'Don't beat me Pa! And I'll … say a Hail Mary for you …' Josephine Murray, the wife of William Murray, treated Joyce with great kindness after the death of his mother; she is one of the most sympathetic characters in *A Portrait of the Artist as a Young Man*. But Joyce's most vivid childhood memories of his mother's family centred on his music-teacher aunts Mrs Callanan and Mrs Lyons. They, along with their home at 15, Usher's Island, are the focus of 'Sisters' and 'The Dead', generally accepted as the two finest stories in *Dubliners*.

Mary Jane Murray and John Joyce were married in the spring of 1880. In the following year their first child was stillborn, but Mary was pregnant again within a few months. On 2 February 1882 she gave birth to her first surviving child at 41, Brighton Square, Ranelagh, County Dublin. James Augusta Joyce, to give him his full baptismal name, came into a comfortable Catholic middle-class background. Ranelagh was one of the more fashionable Dublin suburbs, and the modest brick house in Brighton Square (in reality a triangle) was opulent in comparison to the squalid tenements and artisan cottages of the poorer classes. The new child's first and middle names reflected his parents' aspirations to a higher social standing. He was baptized James Augusta (a misspelling

12

of the intended Augustine) Joyce. The name James had been passed down his father's line for several generations, whilst Augustine was popular as a saint's name for the offspring of educated Catholic parents.

John and May Joyce had nine more children between 1882 and 1894 – Margaret (Poppie) and Stanislaus in 1884, Charlie in 1886, George in 1887, Eileen in 1889, Mary (May) in 1890, Eva in 1891, Florence in 1892, and Mabel (Baby) in 1893. One further child, a boy christened Frederick, was born in 1894, but died a few weeks later. As is common in large families, not all the children were equally close. James was closest to his younger brother Stanislaus, his confidant and supporter during his youth and early manhood, although in later years his sisters Eileen and Eva were to join him in Trieste for a period. During the early years of the marriage John Joyce and his family lived a charmed existence. In 1884 they moved to a larger house at 21, Castlewood Avenue, but within a few years this had grown too small. The next house the family acquired, in May 1886, was at 1, Martello Terrace, Bray, County Wicklow. The small seaside resort, about ten miles south of Dublin, was then in its Victorian heyday. Martello Terrace, a row of fine three-storied houses fronted by a cast iron balcony in the style of those found in the American city of New Orleans, still stands on the northern end of the town's seafront. Joyce's earliest childhood memories were of this house, and it was the setting for the earlier passages of *Portrait of the Artist*. The elder Joyce children had an idyllic time in the spacious house, which was very near to the harbour and promenade. There was a playroom on the third floor, where James and his siblings would perform little sketches and playlets he devised. Stanislaus Joyce's earliest recollection of his elder brother was of seeing him playing the part of Satan in one of these entertainments.

James's complex relationship with his parents, although much modified by the later decline of the family into poverty, began to take shape at this time. He had a special position in the family as the eldest child, the one in whom his parents' greatest hopes were placed. His emotional bond to the gentle but much put-upon May Joyce was very close. She was his 'nice mother', who represented stability, warmth and a safe haven in the world. In his mind she was associated with the purity of the Virgin Mary and the unchanging truths of the Catholic religion. But she was not his alone, and he was forced to share her love with a demanding husband and an army of brothers and sisters. There was an unspoken tension in James Joyce's feelings towards his mother, a hint of jealousy that contributed to his uneasy relationship with women in his adult life. This, it has been surmised, was the source of Joyce's later obsession that he was being sexually betrayed by his life-long partner Nora Barnacle. His father was a drinker and a spender, a musician and a talker, a quixotic and often argumentative philosopher on the nature of life – all traits that his son James would inherit. Stanislaus Joyce, in his memoir of his family, *My Brother's Keeper,* wrote that John Joyce was at home 'a man of absolutely unreliable temper', and, comparing him to James, thought that: 'It is astonishing that a father with so little character could beget a son with so much.' The author was kinder in his own opinion of his ill-tempered father, who had always treated him as his favourite child. 'My father had an extraordinary affection for me,' he wrote after John Joyce's death in 1932 … I was very fond of him always, being a sinner myself, and even liked his faults.

Hundreds of pages and scores of characters in my books come from him.'

Other adults played an important role in the early life of James Joyce, and would afterwards become characters in his books. William O'Connell, James's great-uncle, lived with the family for about six years. He was a pleasant and likeable old man, who got on well with his nephew and often told him about his boyhood days in Cork. Another frequent visitor to the house was John Kelly, a Land League agitator and friend of John Joyce, who regularly spent weekends at the house. Kelly was a gnarled Kerry 'mountainy man', and his ruined hands bore the marks of his many prison sentences for political offences; he appears as John Casey in *Portrait of the Artist*. Mrs 'Dante' Hearn Conway, a large Cork woman, was employed as the children's governess for a number of years. In her youth Mrs Conway had gone to America and entered a convent as a novice. Before she took vows, however, she inherited a large sum of money, and returned to Ireland to get married. Her new husband, who turned out to be a confidence trickster, absconded with her fortune. She was left penniless and reduced to taking domestic employment. Dante was fanatically religious and a rabid Catholic nationalist. Her emphasis on sin, damnation and the devil impressed and frightened James, leaving him with a lifelong fear of thunder and lightning. More prosaically she taught her charges the basics of reading, writing, arithmetic and geography.

James's closest friend in Bray was Eileen Vance, the daughter of one of his neighbours in Martello Terrace. He wrote of her in *A Portrait of the Artist as a Young Man*: 'The Vances lived in number 7. They had a different father and mother. They were Eileen's father and mother. When they were grown up he was going to marry Eileen.' Dante Conway disapproved of Eileen because she was a Protestant, and warned James that God would punish him for playing with her. The two children attended kindergarten together, and she was a frequent visitor to the house. Many years later she still remembered the Joyces fondly, and spoke of their love of music. On Sunday evenings John and the elder children would gather around May at the piano, and happily sing the popular songs of the day together.

John Joyce's spendthrift habits began to cause financial problems, and between 1882 and 1894 he was forced to mortgage eleven of his Cork properties to pay off his debts. In 1888 the financial burden on the family was further increased, when James was packed off to boarding school at the tender age of 'half-past six'. Joyce senior, wanting the best education for his favourite son, sent him to Clongowes Wood College, County Kildare, a highly esteemed Catholic preparatory school run by the Jesuit Order. His parents' parting words to the child, on leaving him at the school, typified their contrasting love for their eldest son. His snobbish father reminded James that his great-grandfather had once given a speech in front of the great Daniel O'Connell at the School, then warned him never to inform on a classmate to the teachers. His tender mother petted the child and wept. She was worried about her son falling into bad company, and warned him to stay away from the 'rough boys'.

Joyce experienced the inevitable bouts of homesickness at Clongowes Wood, but generally settled down well at the Jesuit school. He was several years younger than most of his thirty-seven classmates, and suffered much teasing from older boys. Even at this early age the child was conscious of his family's inferior social position compared to that of the other pupils at the school. In *Ulysses* Stephen Dedalus comments that he told them he had 'an uncle a judge, an uncle a general in the army'. There was minor homosexual experimentation – or 'smugging' as it is called in *A Portrait of the Artist* – amongst the pupils, but none of the systematic torture or abuse endemic in the English public schools of the era. Corporal punishment, or 'pandying' as it was known in the school, was an everyday occurrence; this took the form of smacking the culprit on the palms with a bat. In *A Portrait of the Artist* Joyce wrote of being beaten unfairly a few months after his arrival at Clongowes Wood. The Prefect of Studies, Mr Daly (characterized as Baldy-head Dolan in *Portrait* and in *Ulysses*) wrongly accused the child of deliberately breaking his glasses to avoid doing his schoolwork, and 'pandied' him. The boy responded to his punishment by approaching the head of the College, the Reverend John Conmee, and complaining about the injustice. He won a minor victory over authority when the Rector agreed to 'speak to Father Daly about it'.

Religious teaching and practice dominated the ethos of Clongowes Wood, and Theology and Catholic dogma were its most important subjects. After Joyce was confirmed, taking Aloysius as his saint's name, he regularly attended Communion with his classmates. Like most Irish children he was deeply affected by the Mass, with its rich Latin liturgy, sweet-smelling incense and the priests in their ecclesiastical robes. Although he afterwards rejected the Catholic Church in its entirety, Joyce always acknowledged the profound influence of his Jesuit education. At Clongowes Wood, and afterwards Belvedere, he received his academic grounding from some of the best teachers in Ireland. In later life Joyce referred to himself as a Jesuit rather than a Catholic, and said that the Jesuits had taught him 'to arrange things in such a way that they become easy to survey and to judge'. His teachers awoke his interest in foreign languages, and encouraged a passion for the written and spoken word. He learnt how to memorize long passages of verse and text, a practice he continued throughout his life. In addition to his academic studies he was given singing and piano lessons there, and participated in sporting activities like cricket and swimming, despite his poor physique and already weak eyesight.

All in all Joyce was probably happier at Clongowes Wood than the description of the school in his books might suggest. Even so some of his formative experiences there were unpleasant, and helped mould his excessive fears of physical violence and personal betrayal. One of the most vivid episodes in *Portrait* describes a squabble with a classmate named Wells, who asked James for his prized coffin-shaped snuffbox. After he refused Wells lured him out to the toilets, then pushed him into a cesspool ditch. As a result he came down with a fever and was sick for several weeks. Joyce never forgave this treachery from a friend, and when he told the story used Wells's real name.

Irish life during this period was dominated by one topic of conversation, the political fall of Charles Stewart Parnell following the exposure of his adulterous liaison with Mrs Kitty O'Shea. John Joyce admired the nationalist leader greatly, and one of the most powerful of Joyce's childhood memories was an argument over Parnell that erupted between Dante Conway and his father and John Kelly (Simon Dedalus and John Casey in *Portrait*) one Christmas. This passionate quarrel, which ends with Dante leaving the dinner table and

Mr Casey weeping for 'My dead king' Parnell, took place in 1891, a few months after Parnell's death. James was only nine at the time, but he wrote a poem he entitled 'Et tu Healy', which compared Healy, the Irish politician responsible for deposing Parnell, to Brutus, the betrayer of Julius Caesar. John Joyce was delighted with his son's poem, and printed copies for his friends. Sadly no examples of this precocious poem, the first of James Joyce's published works, have survived.

The death of Parnell preceded a downfall in the fortunes of the Joyce family. His father's position in the Collector-General's administration was abolished in early 1892, and John Joyce was left redundant. From then onwards his only reliable income was a meagre pension of £11 a year, and the family's domestic situation grew steadily worse. James was immediately taken out of Clongowes – leaving his final tuition fees unpaid – and the family moved to a cheaper house in the Dublin suburb of Blackrock. A year later, in 1894, they rented another house at 14, Fitzgibbon Street, in the run-down city centre area around Mountjoy Square, on the north side of the Liffey. During this period James, who was now eleven, did not attend school and instead studied at home. He was already attempting to write a novel (now lost) and composing poems. His transplantation into central Dublin offered new adventures. John Joyce once said that if you placed James in the Sahara desert he would immediately begin drawing a map, and the child soon began mapping his native city in his head. For several months he explored the seedy areas around Gardiner Street and the Customs House, beginning to gather the intimate knowledge of the city he was later to deploy in *Ulysses*.

After a few months in the Fitzgibbon Street house the children were sent to attend the nearby Christian Brothers' School. This was a non fee-paying establishment and the class-conscious John Joyce scorned its working class pupils as 'Paddy Stink' and 'Mickey Mud'. Fortunately he happened to meet John Conmee, the former rector of Clongowes, on the street a few months later. Conmee was now in charge of Belvedere College, a large Jesuit school in Great Dane Street. On hearing of Joyce's financial predicament he generously offered to admit his sons to Belvedere free of charge. As a result, in the spring of 1891 James and Stanislaus found themselves attending one of the finest schools in Dublin. Both boys blossomed under their new Jesuit teachers, and received one of the best secondary educations then available to Irish Catholics. Belvedere prided itself on its tuition in languages, and James studied Latin, French and Italian. His best subject, not surprisingly, was English, and in 1897 he received a £3 prize for the best English composition entered in that year's Intermediate Certificate. His overall academic performance at Belvedere won him an annual scholarship worth £20 a year.

Joyce's achievements at school took place against the disastrous slide of his family down the socio-economic ladder. In February 1894 John Joyce was forced to auction off his remaining Cork properties to pay off Reuben J. Dodd, a Dublin solicitor to whom he owed a large sum of money. Accompanied by James he travelled down to collect the sum, which amounted to several thousand pounds, from his auctioneers in Cork. The journey, along with John Joyce's grief and guilt at parting with properties that had been in his family for decades, made a lasting impression on his son. Almost all of the money was handed over to the moneylender, leaving James with a lifelong grudge against Dodd and his descendants. In the Hades section of *Ulysses* he maliciously referred to an attempted suicide by Dodd's son in 1911, deliberately transferring it to 1904 so it could be included in his masterpiece. The loss of the remainder of his inheritance reduced John Joyce to dire poverty, and his tendency to alcoholism grew more pronounced. All of the small sums he earned from his occasional casual jobs as a calligrapher or an election agent were spent on drink. The death of his infant son Freddie in 1893 mirrored the Cork man's sense of decay and failure. He grew violent towards his wife and on one occasion – recorded by Stanislaus – the police were called after he attempted to strangle her in a drunken rage.

In early 1894 the family were forced to move to a small house in Millbank Lane, in the suburb of Drumcondra. Whilst James was living in this house he fell foul of his classmates, after a teacher pointed out that some homework he had submitted contained a religious heresy. On his way home from school several boys waylaid him, and began interrogating him about his literary preferences. Joyce obstinately stated that he thought Byron was a better poet than Tennyson. But in the eyes of his questioners Byron was 'a bad man'. By way of punishment they threw Joyce against a barbed wire fence and beat him with a stick.

The family's sojourn in Millbank Lane only lasted a few months, and by the end of 1894 James and the other Joyces were living at 17, North Richmond Street, in the area of Mountjoy Square. James's remarkable memory, which if not photographic was certainly unusually retentive, contributed to his vivid recollections of this traumatic stage of his teenage years. It is valid to say that Victorian Dublin provided the landscape of everything he wrote, and provided the rich quarry of sights, sound and experiences from which he hewed *Dubliners*, *A Portrait of the Artist*, *Ulysses* and *Finnegans Wake*. The personalities and dialect of the working-class Dubliners amongst whom he lived provided a backdrop for his novels and stories. Neighbours like Ned Thornton – a tea taster – and his daughter Eveline contributed to characters in these books, whilst minor childhood incidents from Joyce's adolescent years in Millbank Lane inspired stories in *Dubliners* like 'Araby' and 'An Encounter'.

Much of James Joyce's secret inner life from the age of fourteen onwards was dominated by the clash between his growing sexual awareness and his strong Catholic religious beliefs. According to a letter he wrote in 1917 to Gertrude Kaempffer, a women he was unsuccessfully trying to seduce, one of his first moments of sexual arousal was provoked by the sound of his sister's nanny urinating whilst they were out walking one day. Shortly afterwards a minor romp with a young servant girl brought the wrath of the Jesuits down upon his head. Joyce's public face at Belvedere was generally that of a pious and exceptionally serious student, indeed one who might aspire to becoming a priest, yet the suspicions of Father Henry, the puritanical rector of the school, were aroused. He learnt about the incident from Stanislaus and warned James's mother that her oldest son was 'inclined to evil ways'. May quizzed Stanislaus, discovered what had happened, and dismissed the girl from her service. She was unaware that James was racked with a mixture of guilt and pleasure over more serious sexual encounters. On his way home one night, at the age of fourteen, a prostitute on the Quays propositioned him. He paid to have sex with her, and afterwards frequented brothels whenever he could. Joyce had recently been admitted to the Sodality of the Blessed Virgin, and over the coming months was left feeling simultaneously thrilled and debased by his hidden erotic activities.

The dichotomy between the schoolboy's spiritual and carnal inclinations was temporarily healed at the end of November 1896, following a retreat at Belvedere organized by Father James Aloysius Cullen, the Jesuit priest of the nearby St Francis Xavier's church in Gardiner Street. Cullen, the founder of the hugely influential Pioneer Association, was a renowned preacher; his ferocious 'hell-fire and brimstone' sermons struck deep with the sinful student, who was filled with self-loathing at his licentiousness during the previous months. Joyce repented and took himself off to see a priest – the first time he dared to go to Confession since losing his virginity. Rather than risk the wrath of Father Henry at Belvedere, however, he went to a Capuchin priest (who did not know him) in Church Street. Joyce, now duly and safely absolved, threw himself into back into the 'faith'. For several months he prayed constantly, counted his rosary beads and indulged in the ascetic practices expected of devoted Roman Catholics in nineteenth-century Ireland. He was still plagued by carnal thoughts, and realized he was like a spiritual King Canute trying to hold back the unstoppable tide of his sexuality. In the balance of his day-to-day life these needs outweighed his idealistic love for the Virgin Mary. Rather than accede to the Church's religious tyranny in demanding sacrifices he could not make, Joyce stopped attending Mass and rejected its teachings. From now on he would live by his own philosophy, and throw down the twin pillars of Catholic guilt and Catholic hypocrisy that had been ground into him since childhood by the servants of the Church. A profoundly mystical experience in his last year at Belvedere underpinned Joyce's decision to seek his spiritual freedom. Whilst out walking by the sea one evening, probably on the Strand at Bull Island Strand, he saw an attractive young girl with a limp. She was wading in the sea, and lifted up her skirts up to avoid wetting them. In a transcendent flash of spiritual insight, Joyce realized his life's task must be the pursuit of his artistic impulses. He abandoned all thoughts of entering the priesthood.

Freed from the restraints of Catholic 'propriety', the young rebel followed his literary interests. He read the novels of Thomas Hardy, considered 'immoral' in Ireland at the time, and found an idol in the dramatist Henrik Ibsen. Joyce discovered that the Norwegian's iconoclastic attacks on the bourgeoisie appealed to his own growing awareness of and hatred for the hypocrisy of Irish society. His social life during his last two years at Belvedere centred on the home of Richard Sheehy, one of his classmates. David Sheehy, the boy's father and a Member of Parliament, encouraged promising pupils from the school to visit his house at 2, Belvedere Place. His hospitality offered James and Stanislaus a refuge from their own dishevelled home and alcoholic father, and they became regular callers. On Sunday evenings Sheehy and his children would hold a musical soiree, at which the guests were expected to sing or otherwise entertain their hosts. James, with his fine tenor voice and quick wit, became a favourite with the family. He fell secretly in love with Mary Sheehy, but was too shy to tell her of his feelings, instead pouring his passion into poetry. Joyce's youthful crush on his unattainable middle-class love is recalled in Mary's fictional counterpart Emma Clay — the 'lure of the fallen seraphim' — in *A Portrait of the Artist*.

As Joyce struggled through his last year at Belvedere, his inner rebellion manifested itself in his attitudes to Father Henry. Much to everybody's awed amusement he parodied his headmaster's physical quirks in the annual school play. In his school classes he devised complicated theological questions, with the intention of confusing his teachers and asserting his refusal to accept their religious certainties. These provocations nearly backfired on him in the summer of 1898. He was meant to sit a Catechism test on the day before his Intermediate Certificate Examinations were due to begin, but did not turn up for it. Father Henry was incensed by Joyce's insolence, and banned him from taking the important Intermediate Examinations. Joyce was only saved from ignominy when his French master went to the headmaster and persuaded him change his mind. The boy's disdain for his Catholic education was reflected in his final school examinations. With the exception of English, where James submitted a prize-winning paper, his results were poor. For the first time since entering Belvedere he failed to win a scholarship grant for his next year's education. Nevertheless he scraped good enough results to be admitted to University College Dublin, founded in 1853 to provide higher-level education for Catholic students.

James Joyce left Belvedere with ambivalent feelings towards his teachers and his education. On one hand he had loosed himself from the straitjacket of their strict religious upbringing. On the other they had imbued him with the sense of scholarship and unquenchable thirst for knowledge that made the Jesuits the Church's intellectual spearhead. Belvedere's most famous pupil would remain a scathing critic of the intolerant religious nationalism its teachers helped foster in Ireland. But if James Joyce never considered himself a Roman Catholic again, his dedication to pursuing his literary experiments proclaimed him a cultural Jesuit for the rest of his life.

CHAPTER
II

*U*NIVERSITY AND LITERARY ASPIRATIONS

University College Dublin (UCD), which Joyce began attending in the autumn of 1898, could not compare in status with Trinity College, the Protestant university founded in the reign of Elizabeth I. Since 1883 UCD had been administered by the Jesuit order, but many of its professors were Englishmen who had converted to Catholicism during the Oxford Movement. The great English poet Gerard Manley Hopkins, perhaps the most famous of the UCD academics of the 1880s and '90s, was dead by the time that Joyce arrived at the University, and its current professors were comparatively mediocre. About half of them were clerics, but whilst the ethos of the University was profoundly Catholic, many of its courses were secular. Joyce chose to study languages, initially English, Latin, French and Italian. The apathy towards his formal education that had began in his last year at Belvedere continued at university, and he was an inattentive and disruptive presence at many of his lectures. Nonetheless he read constantly, devouring both the set pieces on his courses and the works of other writers who took his attention. These included poets like Dante and the novelists Huysmans, Flaubert and Gabriele D'Annunzio. As yet Joyce had not developed a literary theory of his own, but his energetic trawling through the works of European writers and philosophers contrasted with his cavalier treatment of formal lectures and tutorials.

The Joyces' home circumstances continued to slide. In 1898 the family were forced to leave the house in North Richmond Street. Between then and the middle of 1900 they moved four times, on each occasion to a house and lodging around the north-side suburb of Fairview. The reason for this semi-nomadic existence was that there was no money to pay for rent or their grocery bills. Stanislaus described their home as 'The House of the Bare Table'. James still viewed John Joyce with some affection and humour, even though he was responsible for the family's poverty-stricken circumstances. He told a friend that he had put down his father's profession as 'entering for competitions' on his college application form, since that seemed to be his main hope of getting some money. Like many failures, John Joyce hoped to bathe in the reflected glory of his children, and hounded his favourite son to study harder so that he might enter a good profession. James had a slightly better relationship with his father than did his brothers and sisters, who had come to loathe his bluster and inebriated bullying of their mother. At the least the Joyce family's moves added to the future chronicler of Dublin life's store of recollections of his native city. Amongst these was a horrific incident that occurred at the last of their Fairview addresses, 8, Royal Terrace. The row of houses abutted onto the wall of a convent, and the family's peace was disturbed by the screams of a mad nun locked up inside.

Many of Joyce's contemporaries at UCD would be characterized in his two early prose works, and *Ulysses*. The early

1900s saw the rise of a new generation of Irish nationalists, and Joyce's acquaintances represented a cross-section of attitudes towards independence and how to go about achieving it. George Clancy, one of his closer friends at the College, embraced the inward-looking nationalism of the 'Irish Revival'. He was a member of the Gaelic League and a follower of Michael Cusack, the founder of the Gaelic Athletic Association. Joyce disliked Cusack when they were introduced by Clancy, and later parodied his bigoted vision of Ireland in *Ulysses*. He used Cusack as the model for the 'citizen', the pugnacious customer in a bar in Little Britain Street who symbolizes the one-eyed Cyclops: 'The figure seated on the large boulder at the foot of a round tower was that of a broadshouldered deepchested stronglimbed frankeyed redhaired freelyfreckled shaggybearded widemouthed largenosed longheaded deepvoiced barekneed brawnyhanded hairylegged ruddyfaced sinewyarmed hero …'

George Clancy persuaded James to take up the Irish language, but he soon abandoned his attempts to learn Gaelic. He could not sympathize with the extremist attitudes of Catholic nationalism, which promoted its own narrow culture to the exclusion of all others. In *A Portrait* Clancy appears as Davin, the likeable but rather naïve enthusiast for all things Gaelic who vainly tries to make Stephen embrace his views. Clancy was martyred for his nationalist beliefs in the War of Independence, when he volunteered for the dangerous job of Mayor of Limerick; he was murdered in cold blood by Black and Tan irregulars.

Thomas Kettle represented another strain of the nationalist movement. In his vision Ireland's salvation lay through opening herself to the influences of European culture. 'My only counsel to Ireland' he said, 'is that in order to become more deeply Irish she must become more European.' In 1914 Kettle was amongst the many Irish nationalists who joined the British army in the belief that their participation on the British side would lead to Home Rule for Ireland. Like hundreds of thousands of his countrymen he died on the Western Front, and never saw Ireland become independent. Joyce approved of his friend's aspirations, for he was already beginning to look upon himself as a European first and an Irishman second. Kettle, who married Joyce's adolescent flame Mary Sheehy, treated Joyce kindly when he returned to Dublin from Trieste in 1909. In his later years the novelist might well have sympathized with Kettle's famous comment that 'Life is a cheap *table d'hote* in a rather grubby restaurant, with time changing the plates before you've had enough of everything.'

Joyce considered Francis Skeffington, yet another of his contemporaries whose death could be attributed to Ireland's struggle to free itself from British rule, the cleverest man at UCD after himself. Skeffington, usually referred to as 'Knickerbockers' by his fellow students because of his preference for wearing plus fours, was a true original in the somewhat staid university community. He was a vegetarian, a pacifist, a believer in women's rights, and a dedicated campaigner for various obscure and lost causes. Joyce liked to pick intellectual arguments with his eccentric college acquaintance, but he remembered Skeffington affectionately in *A Portrait,* where he is called McCann. After leaving UCD, Skeffington married Hanna Sheehy, the sister of Mary, and changed his name to Sheehy Skeffington. He took up a career as a journalist and worked to improve the living and economic conditions of Dublin's deprived classes. In 1916, during the Easter Rising, the British army arrested Sheehy Skeffington whilst he was out trying to prevent looting in the city; an insane British officer killed him and three other innocent men in custody.

Joyce's closest friend at University College was a fellow Belvedere ex-pupil, John Byrne. Byrne was a keen sportsman, and as little interested in studying for his degree as Joyce was. Byrne's honesty and refusal to judge others made him the perfect confidant, and Joyce often came to him for advice with his problems. In *Portrait* and *Ulysses* his quiet fellow student appears as the character Cranly. Vincent Cosgrave, in contrast, represented the hedonistic side of Joyce. He was coarse, sharp-tongued, a heavy drinker and a seducer of women. Cosgrave was the dark angel who took Joyce to the brothels behind Amiens Street Railway Station, but there were strong differences in the two men's characters. Joyce did not drink alcohol as yet, and was already unusually prim and proper in his outward demeanour. He found Cosgrave's open vulgarity and sexual boasting irritating, and vainly tried to curb it. The dissolute Cosgrave, interestingly enough, was more aware of the depths and dark places in Joyce's personality and intellect than others. Their later relationship suggests that Cosgrave grew to become jealous of his brilliant peer, and in his mischievous way acted maliciously towards him. Vincent Cosgrave failed to make much of a career for himself in his chosen profession of journalism after leaving college. In 1927, around the time that Joyce was finishing the 'Anna Livia Plurabella' section of *Finnegans Wake* in Paris, Cosgrave drowned himself in the River Thames.

As he progressed through college, and began to master Italian and French, Joyce's literary aspirations began to take a firmer shape. He was by nature rebellious and argumentative, and had little time for the Catholic-dominated Nationalist movement and its idealized vision of Ireland. In 1899 he saw its intolerance in action, when W. B. Yeats's play *The Countess Cathleen* was hissed and booed on its first night by UCD students because they thought it heretical and 'anti-Irish'. Joyce would not join in the attack, and clapped loudly on principle. Shortly afterwards he refused to sign an open letter written by the students of UCD to protest against its portrayal of Irish peasants as 'a loathsome brood of apostates'. In Joyce's eyes, supporting the freedom of the artist was more important than bowing to political, moral or social prejudice. His greatest inspiration at that time was the Norwegian playwright Henrik Ibsen, whose powerful and unflinching social dramas had revolutionized the theatre in the late nineteenth century. Joyce was so impressed with Ibsen's works that he took up literary Norwegian in order to read them in their original language. In late 1899 Joyce read a paper called 'Drama and Life' at the UCD Literary and Historical society. In it he claimed that Ibsen and the other 'new' dramatists had made Greek and Shakespearean drama obsolete. Whilst his ideas were opposed by many of his listeners – who subscribed to the popular view that 'Ibsen is evil' – Joyce's superb off-the-cuff responses to criticisms of his points won him much respect for the breadth of his knowledge and quick thinking.

Not long afterwards Joyce submitted an article on Ibsen's most recent play 'When We Dead Awaken' to the *Fortnightly Review*, a London literary magazine. It was published in April 1900 under the title 'Ibsen's New Drama'. The publisher sent the eighteen-year-old student a fee of twelve guineas for his essay. A fortnight later Joyce was surprised to receive a letter from William Archer, Ibsen's English translator, in which he passed on the renowned playwright's thanks for the sympathetic review. Joyce's distinction in having an article published at such a young age made him even more aloof and self-confident with his peers. He celebrated his small literary success by using the fee to take his father to London for a holiday. Although most of his evenings were spent at the theatre or music hall, he used the daytime hours to call around and introduce himself at the offices of magazines and newspapers. Joyce visited William Archer, who was also an influential critic and unofficial literary agent. In the ensuing years Archer assisted the unknown young Irish writer with advice and introductions to publishers.

Joyce spent much of the summer of 1900 in Mullingar, where his father had been offered temporary employment in the electoral office. There he shocked the residents of the country town by making comments like 'My mind is more interesting to me than the entire country'. He considered himself the coming successor to Ibsen, and wrote a play during his stay called 'A Brilliant Career' – in his own words 'the first true work of my soul'. Joyce dedicated it to 'my soul' but it was only a pale and immature imitation of the Norwegian's masterpieces, and he destroyed it two years later in embarrassment. Joyce sent 'A Brilliant Career' and a selection of his poems off to William Archer in London. He wanted the influential critic's opinion of his work, and secretly hoped Archer might offer help to get it published. Joyce had also begun to compose experimental short prose pieces that he called 'epiphanies', describing moments of transcendent spiritual illumination in his everyday existence. These, he stated, were intended to capture 'the revelation of the whatness of a thing'. Ultimately the epiphanies would be the most important of his youthful literary efforts, since their immediacy and discovery of a deeper meaning in the minutiae of ordinary human lives presaged many of the literary effects he would strive for in his mature works. Joyce later incorporated many of his epiphanies into *Stephen Hero*, the early novel that became *A Portrait of the Artist as a Young Man*.

In October 1901 Joyce's incipient dislike of the inward-looking Irish Literary Theatre was provoked by the discovery that it had failed to include any European plays in its programme for the coming season. He had been translating the German plays of Gerhard Hauptmann, a social realist like Ibsen, in the hopes of persuading the management of the theatre to stage them. Beyond any personal frustrations, however, he believed that the Literary Theatre pandered to its prejudiced audiences by only staging native drama. Joyce wrote a satirical article, 'The Day of the Rabblement', in which he scourged the leading writers of the Irish Literary Revival as provincial, and proclaimed his isolation from 'the multitude'. He submitted this broadside to *St Stephen's*, a new UCD student magazine, and was furious when the college authorities rejected it on the pretext that it mentioned a book on the Catholic Church's banned list. Joyce, as was his habit, appealed to the highest possible authority, in this case Father William Delany, the president of UCD. When the Delany refused to become involved in the dispute he got together with Francis Skeffington, who had also just had an articled censored. They printed the barred pieces as a pamphlet called 'Two Essays', and sold them around the College.

Not all of Joyce's time was spent warring with the College

authorities and the Irish Literary Revival. He kept up his close social connections with the Sheehy family, remaining a regular visitor to their house in Belvedere Place during his time at UCD. With them Joyce displayed a softer, less astringent side of his personality that might have surprised his contemporaries at university. The Sheehys encouraged him to indulge his considerable acting and musical talents, and in 1900 he appeared in 'Cupid's Confidante', a play written by Margaret Sheehy. Joyce took the role of a sophisticated seducer, and received a rave review from one of the Dublin evening papers that he treasured for long afterwards. In February 1902 he went before the Literary and Historical Society to read a second paper, this time on the mid-nineteenth century Irish poet James Clarence Mangan.

Shortly afterward the Joyce family was struck by an unexpected tragedy. George, the youngest of the three Joyce brothers, was a happy-go-lucky scamp who was loved by all the family. In the spring of 1892, at the age of fourteen, he contracted typhoid fever, a common disease in the poorer sections of Dublin in that era. Whilst he lay sick in bed George asked James to come and sing to him. The boy seemed to be slowly recovering, but his doctor started him back on solid foods too early. As a result George Joyce developed peritonitis, and died horribly on 9 March 1902. Joyce mourned his brother in one of his epiphanies. '… Poor little fellow!' he wrote 'We have often laughed together. He bore his body very lightly …' Three years later, in Trieste, Joyce named his firstborn son Giorgio – the Italian version of George – in memory of the fragile younger brother he had sung to on his deathbed.

Joyce left UCD in the spring of 1902, after earning a lacklustre degree that did not come close to reflecting his true academic abilities. He decided to go on to study to be a doctor at St Cecilia's Medical College, but was already more interested in devoting the rest of his life to literature or a singing career. His family had moved several times during his last year at university, and were now living in a small artisan house at 7, St Peter's Terrace, Cabra. Perhaps even John Joyce had grown tired of his wandering existence, since he cashed in half of his pension to buy the property. This would be the home of John Joyce and his family up to the time of James's permanent departure for the Continent in 1904, and beyond.

Joyce was eager to pursue his desire to be a professional writer. His self-confidence was absolute, and he had no qualms about touting his talents to the Dublin literary establishment. Through the artist and writer George Russell, known through his pen-name as AE (who tried to convert him to his theosophical beliefs) James wangled an interview with W. B. Yeats, the leading figure of the Irish Literary Revival. The poet was only thirty-seven at the time, but Joyce viewed him as the representative of an outmoded Irish literary tradition that his future writings would supplant. 'Presently he got up to go,' Yeats wrote in his account of the meeting; 'and, as he was going out, he said "I am twenty. How old are you?" I told him, but I am afraid I said I was a year younger than I am. He said with a sigh, "I thought as much. I have met you too late. You are too old" … The younger generation is knocking at my door…' Joyce's arrogance slightly piqued Yeats, who is said to have described him as a 'Lilliputian literary genius' to a friend. But the remark, if made, was only half-serious, and Yeats, always generous to creative writers, was impressed by the epiphanies and verses that Joyce showed him. He thought sufficiently well of the young man to introduce him to Lady Gregory, the *doyenne* of the Irish literary establishment.

At the end of 1902 the perpetual financial problems of the Joyce family gave James an excuse to cut short his medical studies and leave the stultifying atmosphere of Dublin. John Joyce, having reduced his pension to buy his new house, was now struggling to meet the mortgages he had since raised on it. James announced that he had decided to study medicine at the Sorbonne in Paris, where he could support himself by writing and giving English lessons. He planned his departure, and Lady Gregory wrote on his behalf to the editor of the Dublin *Daily Express,* and arranged work as a book reviewer to help pay his expenses. He left en route for France in early December 1902, and stopped off in London to stay for the night with W. B. Yeats, who had offered to put him up. The poet took him to see Arthur Symons, a literary agent and critic with many connections in France. Symons played a major role in championing Joyce's talents during his long struggle to get his poems and *Dubliners* in print.

Joyce's first trip abroad lasted for only a few weeks. He attended a couple of lectures at the Sorbonne, completed a review for the *Daily Express,* then wrote home complaining that he felt sick. John Joyce raised a second mortgage to pay for James's journey home and he was back by Christmas. But before leaving Paris he visited a brothel, and wrote a picture postcard to Vincent Cosgrave in 'dog-Latin', telling him about the joys of French prostitutes. Simultaneously he bought identical postcards and sent them off to John F. Byrne and his parents; these, needless to say, had innocuous messages. This had an unfortunate repercussion when Byrne met Cosgrave one day and proudly showed off his postcard and the poem that James had written to him. Cosgrave immediately took his matching postcard out of his pocket and read its scurrilous message. Byrne was deeply offended and walked off in disgust, leaving his postcard with Cosgrave. The incident caused a rift between Byrne and Joyce that was never fully healed. Shortly after returning home, Joyce made a new friend in Oliver St John Gogarty, following a chance encounter at the National Library in Kildare Street. Gogarty, who had just returned from studying at Oxford, was in many ways a more talented version of Vincent Cosgrave, and shared his coarseness and blasphemous tongue. Yet he was also a fine writer and on the verge of qualifying as a doctor. Gogarty, a heavy drinker, introduced his new acquaintance to the pleasures of 'grape and grain', and the two medical students whiled away many pleasant hours together in the city's public houses.

In January 1904 Joyce dragged himself away from the dubious pleasures of Dublin and returned to France, intending to continue his studies at the Sorbonne. The second stay in Paris proved somewhat more fruitful than the first. Joyce spent most of his spare time in libraries reading the Greek philosophers, which inspired him to write the 'dagger definitions' of aesthetic terms expounded by Stephen in *A Portrait of the Artist*. He submitted several articles to newspapers and magazines, although his harsh review of Lady Gregory's 'Poets and Dreamers' led E V Longworth, the editor of the *Daily Express,* to suggest he treat the books he was sent to review more kindly. Joyce was still writing verse and epiphanies. Shortly after his arrival in France he sat down and composed two fine poems, 'I hear an army charging upon the land'; and

'When the shy star goes forth in heaven', that reflected his growing maturity and technical accomplishment as a versifier.

Joyce made a number of new friends in Paris, including Patrick Casey, a former Fenian revolutionary who now worked as a typesetter. But his most interesting meeting was with John Millington Synge, whom he encountered on the street one day. Synge was out walking to keep himself warm since he could not afford to heat his room. Joyce's compatriot, who had been living in Paris for several years, was soon to emerge as one of the two great Irish dramatists of the early twentieth century. He told Joyce that he was about to return to Dublin for the production of his first play, *Riders to the Sea,* at the Abbey Theatre, and lent him a copy of the one-act drama to read. Joyce already knew of Synge from W. B. Yeats, and was a little envious of the other man's success in having his work staged. He retaliated by dismissing the masterpiece as 'dwarf drama' and wrote to Stanislaus that he had been 'riddling it mentally till it has not a sound spot'. Yet his criticism stemmed more from envy than a considered opinion of the quality of the play. Joyce later translated *Riders to the Sea* into Italian and was involved in its first performance in Switzerland.

Synge, who had become used to poverty, gave Joyce some sound advice about surviving on his tiny income, and stressed the need for him to eat regularly. Joyce was staying at a cheap lodging house, the Hotel Corneille, and living hand-to-mouth from his articles and by giving English lessons. His small income allowed him an occasional night out to the theatre or music hall, and a copious supply of cheap wine, but little else. Nevertheless he was enjoying his life in Paris and might have stayed longer, were it not for urgent news that arrived from

Ireland on 10 April 1904. That day was Good Friday and Joyce, not withstanding his rejection of the Catholic faith, had gone to Mass at Notre Dame Cathedral, afterwards wandering around Paris for several hours. When he got back to his lodgings there was a telegram waiting. Its stark message was 'MOTHER DYING COME HOME FATHER'. The next day he borrowed some money from an acquaintance and began the boat and train journey back to Dublin.

May Joyce was suffering from cancer, and her death was slow and extremely painful. The memory of his mother's lingering agony left Joyce with such an overriding fear of cancer that in his final months of life he refused to see a doctor because he wrongly thought he had the dreaded disease. May Joyce's death was made harder for James by her attempts to persuade him to return to the Catholic Faith. John Byrne and his aunt Josephine encouraged him to accede to his mother's wish, but James refused to compromise, although he was consumed by guilt at the hurt he was causing her. May Joyce's suffering came to an end on 13 August 1904, after her sons had been forced to lock their raving, drunken father in the spare room. She was only forty-four years old, but had been worn out by poverty, childbearing and her uncontrollable husband. During her last hours there was an unpleasant scene when May's brother John demanded that her children kneel and pray at the bedside. James and Stanislaus, the family's two atheists, refused to bow their heads to a God in whom they no longer believed.

Joyce did not return to Paris after the funeral. Instead he remained at home, where his father was turning into a habitual drunkard. James made desultory efforts to find work, and continued writing articles, but the loss of his mother left him rudderless; she had been his emotional refuge and constant friend. In his grief he turned for solace to Stanislaus, the family member to whom he had always felt closest. James's younger brother was a good foil to him, serious and steady where he was playful and erratic. Stanislaus also recognized and supported his literary talents, encouraging and listening to his ideas and theories. He was a useful source for Dublin gossip and information, and Joyce used snippets he gleaned from their conversations in stories like 'A Painful Case' and 'Grace'.

Joyce had soured his relationship with Dublin's literary establishment by his rudeness and outspoken views, and was now *persona non grata* with the likes of Lady Gregory and the novelist George Moore. When approached by his fellow poet Padraic Colum, he responded by calling one of his plays 'rotten from the core up' and again attacking the Irish Literary Revival. Joyce's disdainful opinions of his fellow writers cost him his employment with the *Daily Express*. Longworth lost his temper at one of his more scathing reviews and ejected him from his office with a warning never to come back. Yet through this unhappy period James continued to write, honing the ideas that would lead to his revolutionary literary techniques. On 7 January 1904 he sat down and wrote a short piece of prose, half story and half memoir, that related incidents from his childhood. He submitted the essay, which he called 'A Portrait of the Artist' to a small literary magazine named the *Dana*, but it was rejected. Joyce decided to expand the piece into a much longer work that would chart his growth to adulthood. He began writing *Stephen Hero*, the novel that a decade later would be reworked into *A Portrait of the Artist as a Young Man*. By this time, he had also assembled enough poems for a book of verse. Most of these were short, spare lyrical pieces, almost song-like in their simplicity, and Stanislaus suggested the title *Chamber Music* as a title for the collection. Shortly afterwards Gogarty took Joyce to visit a free-and-easy widow named Jenny, who was fond of her porter and liked male company. Joyce began reading his poems, but halfway through she got up and withdrew behind a screen, where she urinated in her chamber pot. Her guests thought this was hilarious, and the legend was born that the incident inspired the title of Joyce's first book of poems.

Joyce had more or less abandoned his medical ambitions, and he began looking around for another career to support himself by. For a short while he seriously considered abandoning his writing and becoming a professional singer. Joyce had a superb voice and might well have succeeded in making a lucrative career as an 'Irish tenor', following in the footsteps of the internationally renowned Count John McCormack. In the spring of 1904 he began taking singing lessons, and shortly afterwards appeared in several public concerts. His performances were well received by his audiences, but once again his natural irascibility hindered his progress. In mid-May 1904 he competed at the *Feis Ceoil* in Dublin, the most important musical competition in Ireland. His first two pieces were so immaculately sung that the judge was on the verge of awarding him the Gold Medal, but the third phase of the competition involved singing a piece by sight. Joyce, somewhat surprisingly, could not read music, and angrily walked off the stage, disqualifying himself from the top prize. Nonetheless he was granted the Bronze medal, and received the offer of three years' free tuition by the famous singing master Palmieri, which he did not accept. Next he turned his hand to teaching, and worked for a few weeks at the Clifton Boys School, a small establishment situated in an old mansion in the village of Dalkey, about eight miles south of Dublin. Francis Irwin, the school's headmaster and founder, became the model for Stephen's rabidly Unionist employer Deasy in the 'Nestor' section of *Ulysses.*

Joyce spent much of his free time with Gogarty and Cosgrave, and joined them in forays into the notorious red light district around Montgomery Street, known as the 'Monto' or 'Nighttown'. In this run-down area of Dublin, long since demolished, dozens of brothels and streetwalkers catered to the sexual needs of soldiers from the large English garrison and native Dubliners alike. Within the confines of his limited budget Joyce had transformed himself into something of a dandy, and was often seen parading around the city wearing a yachtsman's cap and canvas shoes, or in a huge overcoat and wide-brimmed hat that gave him the appearance of a Paris 'bohemian'. In 1904 he abandoned the unhappy house in Cabra, where his unbearable father had begun demanding that his two sons find employment, and took lodgings in the house of one of his friends.

The young writer was fond of girl-watching, and often hung around Dublin's more fashionable streets in the hopes of coming across some new beauty. On 10 June 1904 he was walking along Nassau Street when he noticed a tall, good-looking girl with auburn hair walking towards him. Plucking up his courage, he introduced himself, and learnt that the attractive young woman was named Nora Barnacle. Joyce was wearing his yachtsman's cap, and with his bright blue eyes she at first mistook him for a Scandinavian sailor from one of the merchant ships in the port. Nora was twenty years old, and had recently arrived from Galway to work as a chambermaid in Finn's Hotel on Leinster Street. James asked her to go out with him, and they arranged to meet on 14 June in Merrion Square. Nora failed to show up at the arranged time, because she could not get away from work, and Joyce sent a note to Finn's Hotel: 'I may be blind. I looked for a long time at a head of reddish brown hair and decided it was not yours. I went home quite dejected. I would like to make an appointment but it might not suit you. I hope you will be kind enough to make one with me – if you have not forgotten me!' To his relief Nora wrote back and arranged a second date for the evening of 16 June, the next time she was free. Although neither of them could know it, James Joyce and Nora Barnacle were on the brink of embarking on one of the most significant love affairs of the twentieth century. The young chambermaid would provide the missing piece in the jigsaw puzzle of the personal and artistic life of the twentieth century's greatest writer in the English language. She would become her lover's muse and lifelong partner, inspiring him to write about the sexuality and inner life of women with a frankness that no man had yet attempted.

CHAPTER III

*L*OVE AND POVERTY

The woman that James Joyce arranged to go walking with in Ringsend in the summer of 1904 was not like his other female acquaintances. She resembled neither the refined young sisters of his college friends, nor the working-class prostitutes of Nighttown. Nora Barnacle was a Galway woman, the product of a culture that was less stratified and divided by class than Dublin. Her roots, although she might be a town girl, were in rural Ireland, where there was traditionally a certain freedom in sexual matters. The name Barnacle derives from the 'barnacle goose', a seabird that in medieval times was believed to grow in a shell on a tree before dropping into the sea. Today it is probably better known in its various Irish versions, such as O'Kane and Coyne, but the English form was quite common in Galway and the surrounding counties. Nora's father was a baker by trade, but he appears to have been a drunkard, and was eventually thrown out by his wife. He played no part in his daughter's upbringing, which was left mainly to her maternal uncles, the Healy brothers. Michael Healy was a prominent citizen in Galway, and held the important post of Collector of Customs. He was a bachelor and took a great interest in his niece, as did her other uncle, Tom Healy. Nora was born in March 1884, and was the oldest of a family of four girls. The Barnacles were a poor family, but at an early age Nora was sent to live with her grandmother, Mrs Healy, thus avoiding the worst of the hardship endured by her mother and sisters. Contrary to the myth circulated by some of Joyce's admirers, Nora was neither illiterate nor stupid, and was educated until the age of thirteen or fourteen at convent school.

Nora Barnacle was a strikingly pretty girl, and attracted many admirers, even as a child. In 1897, when she was twelve, a sixteen-year-old boy named Michael Feeny, of whom she was fond, died of pneumonia after contracting typhoid. About four years after this event another suitor – a twenty-year-old clerk named Michael Bodkin – died of tuberculosis. Nora believed she was the innocent cause of the second of these deaths. Michael Bodkin went to her house in winter, and stood outside her window in the freezing cold hoping to catch her attention. As a result he caught the chill that led to his fatal illness. The story, when Joyce heard it, made an indelible impression on him. It formed the basis of his short story 'The Dead', the poem 'She Weeps Above Rahoon', and an important part of Molly Bloom's interior monologue in *Ulysses*.

At home, the young Nora was considered an unruly child, although her alleged misbehaviour was probably harmless enough by modern standards. A friend remembered her stealing sweets from local shops, and she liked to wander around the streets of Galway city. After leaving school she worked as a laundress, and began going out with a young man named William Mulvagh. He was her first serious boyfriend, but her uncles disapproved because he was a Protestant, and forbade the couple to see each other. Nora continued to visit Mulvagh on the sly, and Tommy Healy began scouring Galway with a heavy stick, intending to give his niece a thrashing if he found the couple together. In early 1904 he caught her on the way home from Mulvagh's house, and gave her a beating. Nora was not prepared to put up with such bullying treatment, and within a few days had left Galway to work in Dublin. At Finn's Hotel she had quickly been promoted from her job as a chambermaid to work in the bar and reception area.

The day Joyce and Nora first went out together, 16 June 1904, has been immortalized in literary history as 'Bloomsday', the date on which he set the novel *Ulysses*. Their first sexual encounter, on that same evening, was rapid, passionate and short in duration, since Nora had to be back at her hotel by eleven-thirty. She unbuttoned her new boyfriend's trousers and expertly brought him to climax in her handkerchief. Joyce was overwhelmed by Nora's lack of hypocrisy about sex, and attracted by her combination of earthiness and innocence. The lonely Galway girl, on her part, was much taken by the talkative and witty Dubliner. The couple began to see each other regularly, and Joyce was soon forwarding love letters to Finn's Hotel on a daily basis.

Nonetheless he continued his drinking and carousing with Cosgrave. Four days after that first date Joyce turned up drunk at a National Theatre rehearsal in a room in Capel Street. He passed out in a dark corridor, and had to be thrown out after one of the actresses fell over his prone form. On another evening he approached a girl in Stephen's Green, possibly mistaking her for one of the prostitutes who used the park as a place to pick up customers. He quickly discovered the girl was already with another man, who came forward and gave him a severe hiding. Joyce was left with a 'black eye, sprained wrist, sprained ankle, cut chin, cut hand'. Afterwards he blamed Vincent Cosgrave, who was with him, for not coming to his aid. Joyce was rescued by a passer-by named Alfred Hunter, who brought him home and dressed his wounds and bruises. Hunter is accepted as being the original inspiration for Joyce's version of Everyman, Leopold Bloom in *Ulysses*. Like Bloom he was a Jew, and married to a woman who was rumoured to sleep with other men behind his back. Although it is almost universally accepted that Joyce choose to set his novel on the date he met Nora, the original 'Bloomsday' may have been the day Hunter brought him home after the fight – just as Bloom rescues Stephen in the novel.

The young writer's summer was dominated by his growing love for Nora. Their time together was limited by the demands of her job at Finn's, which she told him only allowed her alternate nights off. Nonetheless they wrote to each other almost every day. Joyce's surviving letters to Nora suggest that they talked long and intimately together, sharing their dreams, plans and secret feelings without hesitation. By autumn the bond between them was so deep that Joyce knew he could not bear to be separated from the Galway girl. The relationship was inevitably intense at times, mainly because Joyce was too consumed by guilt about his sexual obsessions to be comfortable with his past activities. He insisted on confessing his previous experiences with prostitutes to Nora, and was deeply hurt when she was appalled rather than rushing to forgive him. His rejection of Christianity also troubled her, and he wrote a long letter explaining his reasons for 'warring' on the Catholic Church. Fortunately the more practical and intuitive spirit of the Galway woman was able to cut through his tortured self-abasement. Her long-term needs were simpler than his; Nora sought a companion, a lover and a father for her children in the coming years. Her common sense balanced out Joyce's self-inflicted confusion and emotional posturing. Nora tied her lover to her side with the iron chains of her trust and unquestioning loyalty, and in doing so saved him to write his masterpieces. Without her presence it is unlikely that Joyce would have found the domestic and psychological stability to avoid being consumed by alcoholism or madness. In return Nora shared the life and achievements of the literary genius who came to rely utterly on her.

Joyce's plans for his future writing career were beginning to take a firm shape. During the summer of 1904 Nora inspired him to write a number of new love poems, three of which were published. Joyce was evolving the framework of a book of short stories that would convert 'the bread of everyday life into something that has a permanent life of its own' and extol 'the significance of trivial things'. His intention to write this collection – which in his mind he had already titled *Dubliners* – was conceived after George Russell offered him £1 to write a short story for the *Irish Homestead*. This periodical magazine, nicknamed the 'pig's paper' by more sophisticated readers, was aimed at the rural farming classes, but this did not deter Joyce from setting his piece in Dublin. He wrote 'The Sisters', a story that had its foundations in the death of a paralysed old priest to whom he was related on his mother's side. Joyce incorporated his younger self as a character in the story, along with his father, whom he disguised as an uncle. 'The Sisters' appears slight enough at first reading, but as the story progresses the deceased priest subtly becomes representative of the moral and intellectual paralysis that the Church has imposed upon Ireland. Joyce wrote two more short stories for *The Irish Homestead* during 1904, 'Eveline' and 'After the Race'.

As Joyce wrote the linked stories that became *Dubliners*, he evolved a very clear conception of what he wished from them. 'My intention,' he wrote to the publisher Grant Richards in 1906 'was to write a moral history of my country and I chose Dublin for the scene because that city seemed to be the centre of paralysis. I have tried to present it to the indifferent public under four of its aspects: childhood, adolescence, maturity and public life. The stories are arranged in this order. I have written it for the most part in a style of scrupulous meanness.' Joyce's stories were couched in what critics have called the mimetic style, expressing themselves through the words and thoughts of their characters rather than as a formal narrative. Joyce's experimentation with the mimetic style was one of the most revolutionary aspects of his literary genius, and helped re-invent the way that novels have been written in the twentieth century.

Despite his small literary successes Joyce was penniless most of the time, and survived mainly on handouts from his friends. His growing frustration at failing to make quicker progress as a writer was directed at the Irish Literary Movement. In August 1904 he submitted an article in verse called 'The Holy Office' to the *St Stephen's* magazine, in which he savaged Yeats, Russell and other leading Irish writers. Joyce, declaring he was seeking a higher literary truth than his hypocritical contemporaries, broke off his connections with them:

> 'And though they spurn me from their door
> My soul shall spurn them evermore.'

Constantine Curran, the editor of *St Stephens*, returned the diatribe as totally unsuitable for the magazine. Joyce then borrowed the money to print it himself, and circulated it around the city.

With the exception of his romance with Nora, nothing seemed to be going right for Joyce. On 9 September 1904 he moved into a Martello tower at Sandycove in south Dublin, which he had arranged to share with Oliver St John Gogarty. The Martello towers were coastal defences erected in parts of Ireland, Britain and the Channel Islands during the early nineteenth century, to guard against an expected Napoleonic invasion. Imposing circular structures, about forty feet high and built of finely cut stone, they dominated the beaches and low cliffs on which they were placed. The tower at Sandycove was magnificently sited on a headland facing Dublin Bay, and like many of its fellows had been converted into a pictur-esque, if cramped, residence. In *Ulysses* it is the starting point for Stephen Dedalus in his journey around Dublin, and has since been converted into a museum dedicated to the writer. But Joyce only lived there for five days. His friendship with the sarcastic Gogarty was always uneasy, and he heartily dis-liked the third tenant, an Anglo-Irishman named Samuel Trench whose blind devotion to Gaelic culture left Joyce in a state of permanent irritation. The tensions came to a head on 14 September, when Trench had a nightmare that there was a panther in the tower. He woke up, grabbed a revolver, and wildly fired several shots. Gogarty took the pistol from him and joined in, aiming in the general direction of Joyce's bed. Apart from dropping some pots on the writer's head they did him no harm, but the prank terrified him. Joyce stormed off in the middle of the night, and walked the seven-mile journey back into Dublin. There he found a temporary refuge with his aunt Josephine Murray; and considered his future options.

For some time he had been thinking of leaving Dublin for Europe, but he wanted Nora to share his 'hazardous life' on the Continent. On the night after the hurried departure from the Martello Tower, he met his lover and asked her to elope with him. Formal marriage was inimical to Joyce's anti-clerical principles, but in effect his words were a proposal. The Galway woman agreed to join in his flight, and the next day Joyce wrote a letter expressing his thanks.

'… Allow me, dearest Nora, to tell you how much I desire you to share any happiness that may be mine, and to assure you of my great respect for that love of yours which it is my wish to deserve and to answer.'

Before the couple could make their escape from Ireland there was much to be done, not least finding the means to support themselves. Joyce answered an advertisement by the Midland Scholastic Agency, an English bureau run by a Miss Gifford, which offered to find teaching jobs abroad for a two-guinea finder's fee. After several weeks she wrote back with an offer of work in the Berlitz language school in Zurich, Switzerland. Joyce had no money for their train and boat fares, and went the rounds of his friends looking for loans. Lady Gregory generously gave him £5, despite his earlier bad reviews of her books, and his open contempt for the movement of which she was patron, and he was able to scrape up enough to reach Paris, where he hoped to borrow more money. Joyce had completed *Chamber Music*, his poetry collection, and wished to submit it for publication before leaving Ireland. On the advice of Arthur Symons he sent the manuscript off to Grant Richards, a small literary publisher based in London.

Joyce did not inform his father that he was taking Nora away with him, fearing he would not approve of his relationship with a common chambermaid. He had not spoken to John Joyce for several months, but went to say goodbye a couple of nights before he left for Paris. His father, not suspecting that James was taking a female companion with him, gave him his blessing. John Joyce approved of his son's decision, and even gave him £7 to help him on his way. Stanislaus and Joyce's sisters knew Nora was accompanying him, as did his aunt Josephine and a number of his literary friends, but they said nothing. John Joyce did not find out until afterwards, even though he went to the docks to see his son off. On the night of 8 October 1904 James and Nora made their separate ways onto the ferry to England at the North Wall and set off on their great adventure. The young woman was making a great leap of faith in her lover, since she had burnt her bridges behind her by running away with him. Several of James's friends, including George Russell and Francis Sheehy Skeffington, pitied Nora; they believed he would inevitably abandon her sooner or later. Behind them the couple left a backwash of rumour and innuendo that endured for years. Decades later Kathleen, the mother of Brendan Behan, expressed the opinion most Dubliners held of Nora's motives for leaving Dublin: 'She was supposed to be in a particular condition when she left Ireland. I wonder, was she, or did she make it up?'

They reached Paris two days later, after a brief stop-off in

London. Their funds had run out, and Joyce left Nora sitting in a public park whilst he went off to get a loan from one of his former language pupils. Two hours passed, and she was beginning to wonder if he had already deserted her, when he returned with their fares to Zurich. On the following morning the couple arrived in the city, and went immediately to book into a guesthouse. Later that day Nora and Joyce consummated their 'marriage'. Up until this point, their physical relationship had been restricted to fondling. For years afterwards Joyce tormented himself about whether he had been the first man to sleep with her. It seems most likely, given the moral attitudes of the era, that she was a virgin at the time; even if she were not, Joyce, who had been consorting with prostitutes for years, was hardly in a position to complain. For a man whose ideas were in many ways 'modern' and who had cast off the irons of his boyhood religiosity, it was a curious obsession. Nonetheless his consuming fears about Nora's past lovers deepened his desire to explore the secret, inner life of women. Joyce's obsession with sexual betrayal and cuckoldry manifested itself most strongly in Molly Bloom's adulterous behaviour in *Ulysses,* and in his play 'Exiles'.

The couple's expectation that they would live in Zurich was rapidly disappointed. When Joyce turned up at the Berlitz School to begin work, he discovered nobody had heard of him; the promised vacancy did not exist. He was in a desperate situation, but fortunately found a sympathetic hearing from the school's director Herr Malacrida, who promised to contact other Berlitz schools for him. Whilst waiting for another teaching post to fall vacant, Joyce spent his free time writing another chapter of *Stephen Hero*. About a week later he was informed that there was a vacancy in Trieste, the largely

Italian-speaking city on the Adriatic Sea that was the Austro-Hungarian Empire's main port. On 20 October, Joyce and his beloved arrived in the pleasant city they believed would be their new home. Once again they were unlucky, for the position had already been filled. Joyce found a few private pupils, but their fees were small, and he and Nora were living on credit. To make matters worse the young Irishman found himself arrested when he intervened on behalf of three drunken English sailors who were involved in a fracas with a policeman. He was soon released, but the rude and offhand attitude of the local consul left him with a permanent dislike for the British diplomatic staff in the city.

Whilst he and Nora hung around Trieste waiting for something better to turn up, James continued writing *Stephen Hero*. He had worked out a careful plan for his literary career, and intended his novel to have sixty-three chapters; *Dubliners* was to consist of ten stories (although he later added others). Joyce was now working on his next story for the collection, originally called *New Year's Eve*, which after many alterations was re-titled *Clay*. Before it was finished he received the offer of a permanent teaching job, at the new Berlitz academy in the seaport of Pola, about 150 miles southeast of Trieste. When his employer, a Signor Artifoni, discovered the young teacher was not travelling alone, he suggested that in Pola he and Nora pass themselves off as man and wife, so they would not scandalize the other staff members or their neighbours. Thus was born the lie that Nora Barnacle and James Joyce were married in the Austrian-held part of Italy in 1904. Pola had been a thriving port in Roman times, but the medium-sized town in which they now found themselves was mostly a late nineteenth-century creation; it was built around a huge arsenal and naval dock that serviced the Austrian fleet. Joyce and Nora rented a small room a few doors down from the Berlitz School, and began to settle into their new home.

The six months that he spent in Pola allowed Joyce to improve his poor Italian with the help of one Signor Francini, a Florentine who taught at the Berlitz academy and befriended the engaging Irish couple. Other employees at the school afterwards recalled that Joyce and Nora were friendly, but extremely poor. They had left most of their possessions in Zurich, and struggled to make do with the few clothes they had brought with them. Nora was soon pregnant, and as autumn turned into winter, she suffered miserably in the unheated flat. Unlike James, who had his teaching and writing to fill the hours, she had little to do with her time but brood. Nora was anxious about their future together, and felt more than a little homesick. She secretly worried about what her family thought of her, and wrote to Stanislaus to ask him if he would call into Finn's Hotel and see how they had reacted to her elopement. Her situation improved in January 1905, when Signor Francini and his wife, seeing how miserable Nora was in the freezing lodgings, offered the couple a room in their heated house.

Joyce did not entirely cut himself off from Dublin, and exchanged letters with Stanislaus and other relatives and friends. His bitterness towards the writers of his home country had not been ameliorated. In 1905, for instance, he obtained a copy of a book called *A Celtic Christmas*. 'What is wrong with all these Irish writers – what the blazes are they always snivelling about?' he complained after reading it. *Stephen Hero* was coming along at a fine pace, and by the end of the year 1904 Joyce had completed nearly seventeen chapters. In

January 1905 he sent off copies to Stanislaus for his opinion, and asked his younger brother to show the manuscript to Vincent Cosgrave and Constantine Curran (the editor of *St Stephen's*). Their positive reaction, when he heard back from Stanislaus, reinforced Joyce's determination to plough his lonely furrow until the novel was completed. Yet try as he might, he found it impossible to interest Nora in his writing. To date their relationship had been progressing well, considering their difficulties, but in this one area he could not move her. Nora was loyal and obviously loved him deeply, yet his intellectual qualities and literary ambitions meant little more to her than the promise of future wealth. Perhaps it was for the best, since if she had voiced even the mildest criticisms or opinions about his art, he would probably have turned against her. As it was they complemented each other in most things, and he was free to follow his literary star without hindrance.

Although Pola had provided James and Nora with a temporary home and an income, the provincial town offered little in the way of social life or entertainment. It was no doubt with great relief that Joyce found himself transferred in March 1905 to the Berlitz Academy at Trieste. According to Signor Francini the move was brought about by an unexpected political crisis. The arsenal at Pola was of great interest to the Italian government, who were bitterly opposed to the Austrian occupation of the region. With the help of local sympathizers, Italian agents set up a large spy ring in the town to keep an eye on their rival's navy. In early 1905 the intelligence operation, involving both foreigners and Italian residents, was betrayed to the Austrian authorities. In retaliation they expelled the nationals of England and other countries sympathetic to Italian claims in the area. Nora and James, who held British passports, were amongst those told to leave. His superior then obtained a post for the banished teacher at the Berlitz School in Trieste. With this move Joyce embarked on one of the happiest and most productive periods of his life. During the decade he would spend in the city of Trieste, he would establish a family with Nora, and at last begin to find recognition as a writer of the first rank.

CHAPTER IV

TRIESTE

In 1904 the city of Trieste was a cosmopolitan mix of Italian, Teutonic and Balkan influences. Today it is a comparative backwater, but when James and Nora arrived there from Pola it was a bustling emporium for the Balkans and central Europe. Although it was predominantly Italian in population, there were also large Greek, Slavic and Jewish communities, and many Austrians employed in administering the city. Trieste, rather like Dublin, consisted of an old town clustered around a cathedral and a castle, adjoined by a new city with an eighteenth-century core. Politically there were similarities as well. Many of Trieste's citizens wished to see the city as part of Italy rather than the Austrian Empire. There was a strong pro-Italian movement called the Irredentists, supported not just by Italians but also by many Jews, who resented the anti-Semitic policies of the Austrian government. Nevertheless Trieste was a far older and more diverse city than Ireland's capital, and the crowds on its busy streets came from many different countries.

On arriving in Trieste the Irish couple found a room in the new part of the city. Joyce soon settled into his teaching job, but did not find his new superiors and fellow teachers as congenial as those in Pola. The owner Signor Artifoni and his assistant Bertelli were petty bullies in his eyes, and he found it hard to hold his temper with them. Nora's pregnancy also caused some problems with his employers, since junior Berlitz teachers were usually expected to be single men. Their landlady, when she realized that Nora was with child, was equally unhappy and evicted them within a few weeks. After huge difficulties James found a room at 31, Via Nicolo, just beside the Berlitz School in the Piazza Ponterosso. The two lovers were not getting on well at this point. Nora was lonely, and resented being left on her own at night, when Joyce would go off with his friends. He had become a Socialist, and spent many of his evenings drinking and talking in the cafés and bars, often returning in the early hours of the morning so drunk he could hardly stand. Nora became tetchy and distressed. She had no great desire to be her uncaring husband's house slave, and felt too tired to undertake domestic chores or cook an evening meal. From then onwards the couple would normally eat dinner out at one of the local restaurants.

The lack of money was a constant problem since neither of them was capable of stretching their meagre income to last for a month. To help alleviate their poverty Nora reverted to the profession she had followed in Galway, and began taking in laundry. Even with this supplement there was not enough to cover the weekly expenses, and James borrowed constantly from the other teachers and his friends in Trieste. He fantasized about making his fortune through a number of imaginative but impractical schemes, including setting up an Italian agency to sell tweeds from the Foxford woollen mills in Mayo. But his ineptness at putting his business ideas into operation equalled his father's. One of his failures involved entering a forty-eight part crossword puzzle competition in an English newspaper, offering a huge first prize of £250. He successfully completed the puzzles and sent them off, only to find he had missed the deadline for entering the competition. Joyce was mired in a frustrating period of his life. In his letters to Stanislaus he wrote of his life as 'martyrdom', and continued to blame the Irish literary movement for his exile. Somehow he continued to write despite his misery, and by July 1905 had completed chapter 21 of *Stephen Hero* and three more stories for *Dubliners* – 'A Painful Case', 'Counterparts' and 'The Boarding House'.

On 28 July 1905, Nora gave birth to her first child, a boy whom they called Giorgio. Joyce proudly sent a telegram off to Stanislaus – 'Son born Jim' – and followed it with a letter giving details and requesting him to ask Constantine Curran to lend him a pound. Joyce was convinced that the birth of his son was the talk of Dublin, and it no doubt caused some unpleasant gossip. The news soon reached his family and friends, causing some amusement to Vincent Cosgrave, who told all and sundry that Joyce's telegram had ended 'Mother and bastard doing well'. He wrote to James to congratulate him, and ended by mentioning that 'Gogarty desires reconciliation'. Not that there was any chance of this, since Joyce bore a huge grudge against his former friend over his departure from the Martello tower in Sandymount. In his books he described the characters he based on Gogarty – for instance Goggins (in *Stephen Hero*), Buck Mulligan and Boylan (*Ulysses*), and Robin Hand ('Exiles') – with a pen dripping in venom.

During the first months of Giorgio's life Joyce wrote five more stories for *Dubliners*, including 'Ivy Day in the Committee Room', 'An Encounter', 'A Mother', 'Araby' and 'Grace'. He had reached his target of twelve stories (although he would later add three more) by October 1905, and sent the manuscript off to Stanislaus for criticism. James intended his portrayal of Dublin to be meticulously accurate in every detail, and asked his brother to verify a list of minor facts in the stories. By early December he was satisfied he had done all he could do with the book and submitted it to Grant Richards, whom he had contacted with his poems before leaving Ireland. The London publisher had rejected *Chamber Music* some months previously, and Joyce was now trying unsuccessfully to place it elsewhere. Richards, after getting over the surprise of finding a book about Dublin arriving from Trieste, liked the stories and decided to publish them. In March 1906 Joyce signed the contract and prepared for the literary fame that seemed at last to be coming his way.

He was to be bitterly disappointed. He wrote an additional story called 'Two Gallants' and sent it off in February, and then another called 'A Little Cloud'. Before he could get in the post he received a letter from Grant Richards informing him that he could not publish the book unless its author agreed to change some sentences. It appeared that the printer of the book had noticed certain passages in the most recent story that he thought were obscene, and proceeded to go through the book marking swear words and questionable state-ments elsewhere. By modern standards the objections were laughable, involving minor issues like the use of 'bloody' or a reference to 'having' a girl. But English literature was still encased in a puritanical straightjacket, and even the mildest deviance from the moral norm in a book could result in a prosecution for obscenity. Joyce stood his ground, and insisted that any newspaper report about a divorce case or criminal assault was more offensive than his Dublin characters' faithfully reproduced dialogue. He pointed out that Richards had made no comments about his story 'An Encounter' (describing a chance meeting between two schoolboys and a peculiar man with an obsession about beating boys). The publisher replied by asking that 'An Encounter' be removed from the collection. Joyce reluctantly agreed to accept some changes, but his attempt to get *Dubliners* into print was turning into a disastrous mess.

The story 'A Little Cloud' reflected something of his dissatisfaction with Nora and his domestic life. The situation of Little Chandler, the young husband trapped in a job he hates and imprisoned in an unhappy marriage, paralleled its author's own feelings of frustration. Joyce, like the protagonist of 'A Little Cloud', was jealous of his child's demands on his wife's love, and felt neglected. He began flirting with several of his female students, most notably an Austrian girl named Anny Schreidner, who was one of his neighbours. Her parents quickly put an end to the budding romance by withdrawing her from the school, but the incident suggests his estrangement from Nora at the time. A letter to his aunt Josephine in December 1905 makes it clear that Joyce was seriously considering leaving, his main complaint being that his common-law wife did not appreciate that he was an artist and not like ordinary men.

James, almost since arriving in Italy, had been encouraging Stanislaus Joyce to leave Ireland and come to live with him and Nora. Stanislaus was unhappy in Dublin, and only his worries about leaving his sisters with his domineering drunkard of a father held him back. Towards the end of the year a vacancy came up at the Berlitz School in Trieste, and James successfully pressed Stanislaus to accept it. By Christmas the brothers were reunited, and Stanislaus had moved into the flat in the Via Niccolo. The three adults and Giorgio got by as best they could in the tiny quarters for several months, until they were again rescued by Joyce's friend Signor Francini, who rented them part of his large apartment in the city.

The presence of Stanislaus helped steady James a little. Compared to his brother Stanislaus was stolid and reliable, a payer of bills and a keeper of schedules. In *Finnegans Wake* James satirized their differing characters in the squabbling brothers Shaun and Shem, but during these early Trieste days Stanislaus curbed his brother's self-destructive drinking and tried to bring some order into his chaotic life with Nora and Giorgio. But even he could not altogether control the couple's excessive spending, their habit of eating out most nights in restaurants, and Nora's fondness for clothes. In May 1906 the Berlitz School notified the brothers that one of them would have to be let go for the summer. James, restless as ever and seeking a new start after his difficulties in Trieste, announced he would step down. He answered an advert from the Nast-Kolb Schumacher Bank in Rome and was granted a two-month trial as a correspondence clerk, at a salary of £12 a month. At the end of July 1905 he, Nora and Giorgio abandoned Trieste and headed for the eternal city, leaving Stanislaus to pay off their outstanding debts.

James's hopes for making a new start in Rome were rapidly dashed. The job was demanding, and he would often have to write 200 or more letters a day. Although the wages were adequate he was paid a monthly salary, rather than by the week as in Trieste, and was incapable of making his money last. To supplement his wages he took on some English lessons in his spare time, cutting back on his opportunities to write. Within weeks of arriving he was sending begging letters to Stanislaus, describing the terrible poverty he was suffering, and asking for loans so that Nora and Giorgio would not have to starve. In fact the entire family had developed huge appetites, and could attribute at least part of their financial hardships to the amount of food they were consuming. Joyce was also drinking heavily again, and in early December his landlady declared she was tired of his drunken antics and evicted the family. Nora found another room, although it was cold and uncomfortable, and they spent a miserable Christmas Day dining on pasta. Nora was pregnant again, and once more alone and friendless in a strange city. But her reserves of strength were growing, and she was determined to keep her common-law husband. She began reading some of the modern masterpieces that he kept mentioning to her, and in early February found a better room where he could write in more comfort.

But Joyce was finished with Rome, which he wrote made him dream of 'death, corpses, assassinations'. He was 'damnably sick of Italy, Italian and Italians, outrageously, illogically sick', and flirted with the idea of going to the French port city of Marseille. In the end he chose to return to Trieste, preferring to risk the devil he knew to the uncertainties of starting over in a new country where he had no contacts. Stanislaus tried to put him off on the grounds that his old job at the Berlitz School was now filled, and suggested he should pursue his banking career. But James hated the idea of such a bourgeois existence, and believed it would lead to 'a great fear of everything inside me' and his 'mental extinction'. In early 1907 he and Nora returned to Trieste, with nowhere to stay and no teaching job on the horizon. Yet for once luck was with them, and they were able to find their feet fairly quickly. After staying with the Francinis for a short while, they found rooms with Stanislaus. The manager of the Berlitz school, Signor Artifoni, who feared losing some of his best pupils if the Irishman set up on his own, offered James some part-time teaching work at the academy. Within a few weeks it was as if the couple had never left Trieste.

In fact the experience in Rome had left its mark on James. Perhaps his unhappiness there had led to a softening in his feelings for the people of his native city. During his stay in Rome he wrote to his aunt Josephine and asked her to send him a map of Dublin, and some photographs of the city. He did little new writing during these months, although he revised 'After the Races' and 'A Painful Case', and toyed with a half dozen ideas for stories. Joyce was seeking to ameliorate the harshness of his portrayal of Dublin by ending the collection with a story showing the generosity of its inhabitants. It can be guessed that the poor and lonely Christmas Day of 1905 sparked the idea of describing a Yuletide evening at the house of his great aunts the Finns, with its traditional ham and goose buffet followed by dancing and musical entertainment. From it Joyce conceived the plot of 'The Dead', the masterful long story with which *Dubliners* is concluded.

Joyce's problems with Grant Richards over *Dubliners* culminated in the publisher refusing the book in September 1906, even though the author was now willing to accept most of the proposed cuts. Joyce was furious and consulted a lawyer, who advised him there was little point in suing Richards for breach of contract. He began sending the manuscript off to other publishers but received no encouragement from them. His disappointment at its rejection was counterbalanced by the news that Arthur Symons had found him a new publisher for *Chamber Music*, which Elkin Mathews had agreed to include in his 'Garland' series of shilling books. Joyce considered that the poems in *Chamber Music* belonged to a now outmoded stage of his development as a writer, and felt they were irrelevant. Still it was one small success to set against his failure with so many other projects, even if he could not expect to receive much money for them. *Chamber Music* was published in an edition of 500 copies in May 1907, but attracted very little interest beyond sympathetic reviews from Arthur Symons and Joyce's former UCD friend, Thomas Kettle. By 1913 it had sold less than 200 copies in all, a dismal showing even for a first volume by an unknown poet. Notwithstanding their commercial failure, there was much to admire in the beauty of Joyce's simple, exquisitely phrased, songlike poems. Indeed it is in musical settings that the haunting quality of poems like 'Sounds in the Earth and Air' can best be appreciated.

In the first half of 1907 Joyce was invited by Roberto Prezioso, the editor of the Trieste evening newspaper *Il Piccolo*, to submit three articles on the political situation in Ireland. Joyce's view of his home country in the pieces (which were published in March, May and September 1906) was tinged with his hatred of the Church and Nationalist movement, but attracted favourable attention from Trieste's irredentists. After the first article appeared he was asked to give a public lecture, and on 27 April addressed a packed hall on 'Ireland, Island of Saints and Scholars'. His cool and somewhat sceptical opinions on his homeland's future, given in near-perfect Italian, were well received by his audience, which consisted mainly of Berlitz students. Nonetheless Joyce was frustrated with Italy, and made enquiries about emigration to South Africa. Apart from his work on 'The Dead' he was writing little, and he was tired of his cramped domestic arrangements. But in the summer of 1906 two events took place that put an end to any plans to leave Italy. In July, James was taken ill with a serious attack of rheumatic fever, which kept him in bed until September. He was still in hospital on 27 July, when Nora gave birth to their second child, a girl who was named Lucia Anne (Joyce had chosen the first name, after the patron saint of eyesight, some years previously). In the crisis Stanislaus once more came to the rescue, and provided financial support whilst his brother was unable to work. But the months of sickness provided Joyce some space to think about his future, and renewed his determination to reforge *Stephen Hero* into a more suitable form.

By the end of September, Joyce had completed 'The Dead' and was beginning to rewrite *Stephen Hero* as *A Portrait of the Artist as a Young Man,* turning its twenty-eight short chapters into five long sections. When he recovered his health and returned to the Berlitz School, he learnt that two of the teachers had taken it over. The long-suffering Stanislaus was left with the burden of paying his brother's medical bills, which the previous owner of the school had agreed to cover, then reneged on. Joyce, rather than go back there, decided he would make more money by taking private pupils. His control over his finances did not improve with the new arrangement. Nora, who was left to deal with the results of his carelessness with money, finally began to lose patience with their hand-to-mouth existence. Joyce rarely paid his debts, leaving her to face angry creditors, and she grew into the habit of taking money from him surreptitiously to pay the more angry creditors. Unfortunately this often left the family with no money for food. By 1908 Nora, who was once again pregnant, was angry enough to threaten to write to her relatives telling them her husband wasn't man enough to support her, and demanded that he curb his drinking. At the end of that year Stanislaus noted in his diary that he had saved the family from starvation six times. Joyce was worried about his eyesight, which had been troubling him since his bout of rheumatic fever, and after a few false starts, he temporarily renounced alcohol. In August 1908 Nora lost her baby, to the distress of her husband. In *Ulysses,* the sorrow that haunts the mind of Leopold Bloom is the death in infancy of his son Rudy.

During his worst bouts of poverty Joyce was often saved by loans from his pupils. His friendships with some of them were very close, and reveals an appealing side of his personality that is sometimes lost in recounting the upheavals of his literary and domestic life. Joyce was an entertaining, if eccentric, teacher, and once they achieved a level of competence in the English language his adult pupils came to enjoy his amusing company. The most interesting of his regular students was Ettore Schmitz, the middle-aged Jewish manager of a paint factory. Joyce was interested to discover that Schmitz had written two novels in his younger years. They had both failed to attract any interest, but on reading them Joyce found himself impressed by their insight and humanity. In return he showed the factory manager the first chapters of his re-writing of *A Portrait of the Artist as a Young Man,* and asked for his comments. Schmitz replied with some friendly but incisive criticisms that led Joyce to make some minor changes in the book. Throughout the remaining Trieste years the factory manager and his wife Livia helped Joyce, although the difference in their social stations was such that Mrs Schmidt would not acknowledge Nora (who did her laundry) when they met on the street. Ettore Schmidt, with Joyce's encouragement and help, began writing again, and under his pen name Italo Svevo later established himself as one of the greatest Italian novelists of the first half of the twentieth century.

In early 1909 Nora and James Joyce moved to a more comfortable apartment at 8, Via Venetio Scuosa. Stanislaus did not accompany them, having been insulted by his brother during a row about his unpaid bills. They were reconciled when James apologized for his rudeness, but their fraternal closeness was a thing of the past. Joyce was restless and frustrated. Lucia was a difficult child and her constant crying made it hard for him to write. After finishing the first three chapters of *Portrait* by April 1909, he found himself unable to progress any further, and stopped working on it. Joyce's troubled spirit was turning back to Dublin, and his severed emotional ties with his family and friends. John Joyce, for all his bitterness at the elopement, missed his favourite son and yearned to see his grandchildren. There was also the hope of finding a publisher at home for the still unplaced *Dubliners*. Joyce was corresponding with Joseph Hone, of the firm of Maunsel and Co. in his native city, who had expressed a firm interest in the book. At the end of July 1909 he returned with Giorgio to Dublin, leaving Nora and Lucia behind him to be supported by Stanislaus in his absence. It was the first time that the couple had been separated for more than a few days since their elopement in 1904.

Joyce's return to Dublin brought on the greatest crisis of his life to date. At first things went as he had planned, and on turning up at his family's squalid house in Fortenay Street (the house at Percy Place had been sold to cover more debts), he found his sisters overjoyed to see him. The next day he went alone with his father for a walk in the country, and made his peace with him. Dublin is a small city, and Joyce soon encountered many of his old UCD friends and enemies. He learnt that Thomas Kettle was about to marry his former sweetheart Mary Sheehy, and made a grudging (on his part) reconciliation with Oliver St John Gogarty. His initial meeting with his old acquaintance George Roberts, the managing director of Maunsel, went well, and left him satisfied he would soon be in print. Before Joyce left Ireland the publisher gave him a signed contract for *Dubliners,* and an advance of £3 on royalties.

But, as so often happened in Joyce's life, a seeming triumph was rapidly followed by an unexpected catastrophe. On the afternoon of 6 August, about a week after his arrival in Dublin, a conversation with Vincent Cosgrave brought the unsuspecting writer almost to the brink of insanity. Joyce had been spending a lot of time with Cosgrave, who was still living the rootless carefree existence of their student days. On this particular day the conversation turned to Nora, with whom the medical student had been closer than most of Joyce's friends. Cosgrave suddenly informed him that in 1904, on the nights when Nora was supposedly working in Finn's Hotel, she had in fact been with him. Joyce was horrified. He rushed off and wrote a tortured letter to his common-law wife accusing her of betraying him. The next morning he wrote to her again, this time demanding to know if she had been a virgin when they met, and questioning whether Giorgio was his child. For two days the distraught writer wandered around Dublin in a dream, unable to carry on his business or face any of his friends. Then, on the afternoon of 8 August, he went to the house of John Byrne at 7, Eccles Street, and poured out his story. Byrne heard him out, then declared that in his opinion the story was a 'blasted lie'; he guessed that Cosgrave and Gogarty had made it up because they feared what he was going to say about them in his books. Joyce seized on the unlikely explanation, which appealed to his own latent paranoia and delusions of persecution by all around him. He began to gain some stability over himself and feel ashamed of his anger towards Nora.

In Trieste, meanwhile, Nora had received the letters and was stunned by their tone and contents. She showed them to Stanislaus, and in a state of anguish and confusion asked him what she should do. As so often over the years Joyce's younger brother intervened to help smooth things over between the couple. He wrote telling James that during the summer of 1904 he remembered meeting Cosgrave in a Dublin pub, who told him he was depressed after just being rejected by Nora. On receiving this information Joyce's doubts were stilled, and he wrote letter after letter to Nora to tell her of his renewed love. He begged her to forgive him for believing Cosgrave's lies. It is impossible to gauge whether there was any truth in the suggestion Nora had pursued a romance with Cosgrave, or if indeed the accusation was ever made. Joyce was so tormented by jealousy that he could quite easily have responded irrationally to a perfectly harmless joke or comment. Cosgrave was well aware of Joyce's susceptibility. On the other hand it is possible that Nora had a small fling

with the personable Cosgrave in the early days of her romance with James – although everything that is known about
her character suggests that it would not have amounted to
much. The real importance of the incident, however, lay in its
importance to Joyce as a husband and writer. It was part of
his nature that he could only express his deep love for Nora
through his jealousy and doubt. In the short run the accusation and its passionate retraction revealed to Nora the depth
of his feelings, and rekindled the faded passion between them.
But Joyce's obsession with marital betrayal, already presaged
in the last pages of 'The Dead', would later be expressed both
in his art and his life. His suspicions about Nora's faithfulness,
no matter how unfounded they may have been, would be
resurrected in works to come, particularly in *Ulysses*. In that
masterpiece Joyce's adulterous heroine Molly Bloom lives at
7, Eccles Street, the house where in 1909 John Byrne eased
Joyce's fears about Cosgrave.

Before returning to Italy Joyce took Giorgio to see Nora's
family in Galway. This potentially difficult visit went well,
and he found Mrs Barnacle and her brothers the Healys far
more welcoming than he had expected. Back in Dublin again,
the misery of Joyce's sisters moved him to try to help them.
He arranged for Eileen, a fine but untrained singer, to have
music lessons, and on impulse offered to bring one of the
other sisters back to Trieste with him. The choice fell on Eva,
a quiet and very religious girl, who was suffering from severe
tonsillitis. James used his advance from *Dubliners* to pay for
her to have an operation. On 9 September, five weeks after
his arrival, he left Dublin with his son and sister for Trieste.
Joyce was now twenty-seven-years-old, and had little to show
for his years of writing except an unsuccessful book of po-

ems. With the acceptance of *Dubliners* it now seemed that his stunted literary career was at last about to take an upswing. Instead he would find more years of agonizing frustration, and almost abandon the writer's craft before he began to receive any recognition.

CHAPTER V

'IRELAND MY FIRST AND ONLY LOVE'

Joyce's return to Trieste proved to be brief, although his reunion with Nora was a joyful one. When he gave her a gold pendant, inscribed with the words 'Love is unhappy when love is away', Stanislaus, having carried the burden of supporting her and the two children for weeks, muttered 'So is love's brother'. Yet within a few weeks James was planning to go back to Dublin and pursue what he believed was a gold-plated business opportunity. The new scheme came to his mind when Eva went to a cinema in Trieste one day, and afterwards mentioned it was strange that there were none in a big city like Dublin. Joyce immediately decided that here at last was a way to make his fortune. The film industry was still in its infancy, but Trieste and most European cities had cinemas. The whole of Ireland, on the other hand, could not boast a single movie house, and films were shown only in venues like church halls and meeting rooms. It was a huge omission that promised good profits to whoever took advantage of the opportunity. James approached a syndicate of businessmen who ran cinemas in Trieste and Bucharest, and persuaded them to send him back to set up Ireland's first cinema. He was back in Ireland by 21 October, and within a week had acquired premises in Mary Street, off the city's main thoroughfare, Sackville Street. In November two of his Italian partners arrived in Dublin to oversee the setting up of the cinema. Joyce installed them in Finn's Hotel, where Nora had been working when they met, and asked the staff if he could see the rooms where his wife once worked and slept.

Joyce's common-law marriage had taken a strange turn. After the anguish over his 'betrayal' by Nora during his earlier stay in Dublin, the couple began to exchange letters stating their love and desire for each other in the most explicit sexual fashion. The correspondence was continued during his second stay in the city. Joyce's letters to Nora from this period still survive, and are known to Joycean scholars as the 'dirty letters'. Their eroticism spans the whole gamut of sexual experience, and they are sometime lyrical but often crude and obscene in their blunt images. In many of his letters Joyce displays an obsessive interest in the urinary and excretory bodily functions, whilst others display sadomasochistic trends. Nora's side of the correspondence unfortunately has been lost, but references in Joyce's letters suggest that hers were as open as his own, and full of the explicit sexual words that he winced to hear spoken but craved to see on the written page. The letters, instituted by Nora in an attempt to shore up the marriage after the Cosgrave debacle, reveal much about Joyce's tortured sexual nature. Nora's lack of inhibition in discussing her sexual desires and needs certainly provided the raw material from which he created Molly Bloom. Whatever needs were fulfilled for the couple by the dirty letters, they did not continue after December 1909. About that time Joyce reached a crescendo of sexual vulgarity and crudeness, then as Christmas approached, reverted to the tender love letters that he had hitherto sent to his common-law wife. He and Nora never wrote to each other in this way again.

Not all of their correspondence was erotic in intent. Joyce was still suspicious of Nora, and found her difficult to fathom. 'Are you with me Nora, or are you secretly against me?' he wrote to her. 'I am a jealous, lonely, dissatisfied, proud man.' Many of Nora's complaints about Jim, as she invariably called him, concerned his failure to support her and the children. His reluctance to send money from Dublin angered her, and she was permanently unhappy about their unmarried state. On Christmas Eve of that year, when he at last forwarded her some funds, she replied by sending him a blank wedding invitation, a hint that he pointedly ignored.

The cinema project consumed most of Joyce's days, and he worked long hours to set up the building in Mary Street. It was going to be called the Volta, a name the syndicate had used for their cinema in Bucharest, the Romanian capital. In early December he brought his partners to Belfast and Cork to look for premises for cinemas in those cities also. They were unable to find anything suitable, although Joyce was much impressed by Belfast's thriving linen factories. After some delays the Volta, Ireland's first cinema, opened on 20 December. There were three silent films on the programme – 'The First Paris Orphanage', 'La Pourponniere' and 'The Tragic Story of Beatrice Cenci' – and a string quartet providing a musical accompaniment. Despite enthusiastic reviews the cinema did not do as well as expected. Joyce did not wish to stay in Dublin to manage it and returned to Trieste in early January. Some months later the syndicate realized the venture was a failure; the Volta's manager, a man named Novak, sold the cinema at a loss to an English cinema chain. Joyce, to his great annoyance, received nothing for his work since his partners had made no profit from it.

Before he departed from Ireland Joyce also pursued his long-held ambition of selling Irish tweeds in Trieste. He called on the Dublin Woollen Company beside Dublin's 'halfpenny bridge' and secured an agency. In later years he claimed to have succeeded in clothing several of his Italian friends in Irish tweed suits. His sister Eileen, who hoped to pursue a career as an opera singer, also returned with him to Italy, adding to the financial burdens on his impecunious household. Back in Trieste, Stanislaus was reaching the end of his tether with his brother. All of his wages were being consumed by supporting James and his entourage, and he received no thanks for his efforts on their behalf. He felt that James and Nora were ostracizing him, whilst using him to pay for their extravagant lifestyle. Stanislaus was now living in his own room, but usually ate with his brother and sisters in their chaotic flat. For a short while he stopped doing this, fed up by the erratic times at which he was being fed and by Joyce's refusal to join him at mealtimes. Although Stanislaus resumed eating at the flat after a promise that his treatment would improve, his relationship with his brother and Nora continued to deteriorate.

The years between 1910 and 1912 were the most frustrating that Joyce had yet known so far as his literary career was concerned. His eyesight suffered further deterioration from iritis in the month after the second trip to Ireland, and he was unable to resume his re-writing of *Stephen Hero* into *Portrait*. The three-fifths completed revision was left wrapped in a cupboard, abandoned if not altogether forsaken. Joyce was having as many problems with Maunsell and Co. over passages in *Dubliners* as previously with Grant Williams. Throughout 1910 and 1911 letters about the book flew between Dublin and Trieste, with George Roberts demanding niggling changes and omissions in story after story. Most of his objections concerned references to real people mentioned by Joyce in the stories. Roberts, appearing to think that everybody mentioned in the book was liable to sue him, demanded a cash indemnity from the author. The final provocation came when he objected to a harmless reference to King George V in the story 'Ivy Day in the Committee Room'. Joyce was so incensed that he promptly sent a copy of the story off to the English court with the disputed passage marked, and asked if His Majesty found it offensive. The royal response was to refuse to give an opinion. Joyce, driven to fury by Roberts' refusal to make any final decisions on these various disputes, finally took the strange step of writing an open letter, which was published on 17 August 1911 in *Sinn Fein*, the periodical edited by the nationalist leader Arthur Griffith. In it he outlined the history of his problems in finding a publisher for *Dubliners*, and publicly agreed to make the requested changes, whilst condemning the forced bowdlerization of his text. 'I hereby give Messrs Maunsell publicly permission to publish this story with what changes or deletions they may please to make,' he wrote, 'and shall hope that what they may publish may resemble that to the writing to which I gave thought and time.' Even this missive did not seem to bring the endless delay in publishing the book to a successful conclusion.

The sense of failure in getting his work published culminated in a self-destructive gesture, which if successful, might have ended Joyce's literary hopes. One morning, during a furious row with Nora, he grabbed the manuscript of *Portrait* and threw it into the fire. As the result of years of his pains-taking examination of his early life began to sizzle and burn, Eileen came in and rescued the pages from the fire, burning her fingers as she did so. Once his fury had subsided Joyce thanked her for her selfless action, and told her that he would never have been able to write the book all over again. Eileen was settling well in Trieste and would stay in the city. She had become closer to Nora than James's other sisters, and had a deep fondness for her niece Lucia, whom many people found a strange and unsettling child. The less adaptable Eva, on the other hand, was unhappy in Trieste, and homesick for Dublin. She went back to Ireland in July 1911, preferring to face the misery and hardship of life with her father than an uncertain future in Italy. Shortly afterwards Mabel (usually called 'Baby'), the youngest of Joyce's sisters, died of typhoid, as a direct result of her family's impoverished circumstances.

At some stage in 1912 Joyce and Nora embarked on another of the bizarre adventures with which they occasionally spiced up their uneasy relationship. Joyce was well aware of his wife's striking beauty, and her sexual appeal to other men in Trieste. His consuming jealousy towards her was paralleled by a masochistic compulsion to place himself in the role of the cuckolded husband. He discreetly began encouraging her to pursue flirtations with other men, and afterwards tell him about them. Nora, like any other woman, enjoyed being desired, and began flirting with Roberto Prezioso, a journalist who had been one of Joyce's closest friends since he arrived in Trieste. Although he had a wife and two children, and was also rumoured to be a bisexual, the newspaperman took the bait eagerly. He wooed his friend's common-law wife with gifts and promises, and as agreed she dutifully reported his advances to her husband. It was a dangerous game: Joyce soon began to suspect that the sensual Nora was enjoying it far too much for his liking. He intercepted Prezioso on the street one day and angrily demanded to know what he thought he was doing with Nora. The surprised journalist broke down and began weeping and begging for the aggrieved husband's forgiveness. Joyce gained a sordid little victory over Nora and Prezioso, but in cutting off his friendship with the journalist he lost one of his best contacts in Trieste.

Nora was not alone in seeking romance outside the marital home. Joyce had a number of attractive young female students, and during this period became infatuated with Amalia Popper, the daughter of a rich Jewish merchant. His involvement went no further than erotic fantasies and passionate gazes, but he celebrated his feeling with a number of poems (later published in *Pomes Penyeach*) and a half-satirical, half idyllic prose piece he titled 'Giacomo Joyce'. This short effort, discovered and published after Joyce's death, is notable for being the only one of his works based in Trieste. Joycean scholars suspect that Amalia Popper was the inspiration for Molly Bloom's exotic Mediterranean beauty. Yet the unconsummated romance, like others that followed in later years, was the escape valve of a hopelessly married man. Joyce had made himself emotionally dependent on his wife, to an almost unhealthy degree. The extent of his need for Nora was made clear in July 1912, when she took Lucia back to Ireland to visit her Galway relatives. It was the first time that Nora had returned to her birthplace since leaving to work at Finn's Hotel in 1904. Joyce, left behind with Giorgio, said he looked forward to being in a house without women. But within a week he was utterly miserable without Nora. He borrowed some money from Ettore Schmidt, and pursued Nora to Ireland, accompanied by his son.

The couple's short stay in Galway was one of the most pleasant interludes of their long life together. Nora somehow managed to persuade her mother and uncles that she was now married – although James's principles would not allow her to wear a wedding ring. She was welcomed back with open arms by her relatives and their friends. After her husband's unexpected arrival they visited the Aran Islands together, after which James wrote two articles for the *Piccolo* newspaper in Trieste. Joyce was haunted by Nora's experiences during her Galway childhood. He borrowed a bicycle and rode off to the cemetery at Oughterard in Connemara, the burial place of Michael Furey in 'The Dead'. Michael Bodkin, the admirer of Nora's whose tragic death inspired the story, was interred in Rahoon cemetery in Galway. On 20 August 1909 Joyce composed 'She Weeps Above Rahoon', which, with the possible exception of 'Ecco Puer' remains his finest poem. In its three short verses, each only four lines long, he visualized Nora hearing her dead lover's voice calling her 'At grey moonrise'.

The interminable squabble with George Roberts over *Dubliners* was reaching a climax. The publisher now demanded that 'An Encounter' be removed entirely from the book. Joyce turned to some of his friends for help, but none of them would take his part in helping bring a book that did not portray Dublin as a rosy heaven into print. Even Thomas Kettle, who had been the other boy present when Joyce met the lurking figure described in 'An Encounter', thought that its outspokenness was beyond anything he had ever read. Joyce accepted defeat, and agreed to delete the story, but Roberts immediately came up with more objections. The author could take no more and refused. Roberts declared he would not publish the book, and offered to sell Joyce the already printed sheets of the book for £30. The writer decided to publish the book himself, choosing the Liffey Press as the name of his imprint, but before he could close the deal Roberts's printer became involved in the imbroglio. He declared that as far as he was concerned the book was an insult to Ireland and refused to take any fee for working on it. Instead he was going to destroy the sheets, which he proceeded to do on 11 September. The printer's wilful action left Joyce consumed with anger.

During his weeks in Dublin he had strengthened his acquaintance with the poet Padraic Colum, and began a long-lasting friendship with James Stephens, the diminutive writer whose best-known works today are *The Crock of Gold* and *The Charwoman's Daughter*. Otherwise the literary and social establishment ignored Joyce. He left Dublin with Nora on the same night that *Dubliners* was destroyed, carrying a full set of proof sheets that he hoped to hawk to another publisher. Otherwise he had achieved nothing of any practical value during his stay. He would never return to Ireland. Whilst crossing Europe by train on his way to Italy, James got out his contract from Roberts. He savagely satirized the publisher in some doggerel verses, which he scribbled on the back of the worthless document. Two lines from this poem, which he called 'Gas From a Burner', encapsulated his hatred for the attitudes that lay behind his own country's rejection of his book:

'Oh Ireland my first and only love
     Where Christ and Caesar are hand and glove.'

James Joyce was not the first Irish writer to be driven away by his homeland's bigotry and hypocrisy, nor would he be the last. But he was the greatest, and the most honest. As a man he was selfish, argumentative and paranoid, with an unfathomable urge to bite every hand that fed him. Yet when he took up a pen to write, his unbending obstinacy was transformed into an uncompromising clarity. In every word Joyce wrote he was true to his personal inner vision, and he saw the city of his youth, which he knew so intimately inside his head, without fear or favour, and a considerable colouring of malicious satire. In time the society that rejected him would find itself measured against the slide rule of his literary vision.

Joyce and his family returned to Trieste in September 1911, moving into a new apartment in the via Donato Bramante. They had been evicted from their previous home during their absence for non-payment of rent, and Stanislaus had been forced to save their furniture and find another apartment for them. At first they were destitute, but Joyce was fortunate to acquire a post teaching at the Scuola Superiore di Commercio Revoltella, Trieste's commercial high school. The job left him free to take private pupils in the afternoon. For almost the first time the family achieved a degree of financial comfort, although they remained in the habit of evading their creditors. James was respected by the more enlightened of Trieste's citizens as a teacher, journalist and lecturer on his native country. His dapper figure, with its moustache, *pince-nez* and walking cane, was a familiar sight in the cafés and theatres of Trieste.

Nora had matured into a sophisticated and well-dressed woman, and although shy around her husband's intellectual friends, drew much attention for her startling beauty. Those who got to know her better found that she had a simple charm and a warm sense of humour. The portrait painter Tullio Silvestre, commissioned to paint her portrait in 1913, said he considered her the most beautiful woman he had ever seen. Their higher income allowed some luxuries, and the couple furnished their home with good quality imitation Danish furniture and bought a grand piano. Joyce had obtained some old family portraits which his father had somehow preserved, and he framed and hung these on the wall. The Joyces and their two handsome children were at last attaining the middle-class respectability they craved.

Joyce continued to write occasional poems, but for the moment the creative urges that had driven him in his younger years were muted. Then, in November and December 1913, two letters arrived that at last promised some recognition after his earlier literary failures. The first came from the publisher Grant Richards, to whom Joyce had written after the disaster with Maunsell and Co. Richards felt a twinge of conscience at letting the writer down by dropping *Dubliners* in 1906. He was now prepared to risk publishing the book, especially since Joyce's proof sheets would reduce his costs. After the usual delays it was eventually published on 15 June 1914, receiving good if not ecstatic reviews. The book was not a success at first, and sold only 499 copies in its first two years, one short of the number that had to be sold before its author started to receive any royalties. The commercial lack of success did not reflect upon its importance as an artistic work. The collection showed a mastery of the short story comparable to Chekhov's. Joyce was well aware that the book transcended its narrow Dublin setting. Many years later when the stories were translated into French, it was suggested that they should be titled 'How they are in Dublin'. Joyce replied '*Dubliners* is about how we are everywhere – it is the experience of modern urban life.' Nonetheless the book's greatest influence was in Ireland, where many young writers were overwhelmed by its treatment of childhood, its naturalistic dialect, and the deep insight that underlay Joyce's epiphanies of everyday life. The Irish followers of his literary trail-blazing were to produce some of the greatest short stories of the twentieth century.

The second letter came from Ezra Pound, an American living in London. Pound was already a high-profile figure in literary London, and would emerge as one of the most important English-speaking poets of the twentieth century, but his letter was a request for prose and poetry for several small literary journals and two American magazines with which he was involved. He had come by Joyce's name through W. B. Yeats, with whom he was very friendly at the period. For Joyce it was a godsend, since there were few men more likely to understand his work or to know where to get it published. Pound combined influence with an eye for real literary talent, and during 1913 and 1914 was instrumental in helping the careers of the poets Robert Frost and T. S. Eliot. Joyce sent off the three completed chapters of *A Portrait of the Artist as a Young Man* and a copy of *Dubliners*. Pound brought the unpublished chapters to a small journal called the *Egoist*, founded and managed by a feminist and former Theosophist, Helen Marsden. She was as impressed as he was by what she read, and agreed to publish them in serial form. Starting on 2

February 1914, *Portrait* began appearing in the *Egoist*. By a happy coincidence, this date was Joyce's birthday; he set considerable store by such things.

Joyce had not yet completed his autobiographical novel, but now with the looming target of a monthly deadline he threw himself back into his writing. By mid-1914 he had completed the book. *A Portrait of the Artist as a Young Man* may be described as the literary equivalent of an artist's self-portrait, with the rider that it is retrospective and depicts a younger self. In that sense it is both art and historical document, a personal interpretation of the experiences that made its author who he was, but done from a maturer and more experienced standpoint. But it also carries a simple but important message, namely that the forming human spirit must examine, weigh and be ready to reject the values of the individuals and institutions that try to mould its beliefs. The name of his hero, Stephen Dedalus, symbolically reflects this theme. Stephen was the first Christian martyr, the man tied to a tree and shot through with arrows for his beliefs. Dedalus, the mythical Greek hero, built the labyrinth of King Minos, and was then imprisoned in it. He escaped by building wings of feathers and wax and flying away, but his son Icarus flew so close to the sun that his wings melted and he fell into the sea. The five chapters of the book, each covering a different period of its author's life, begin with his early childhood, and take us through his school days at Clongowes and Belvedere, his religious crisis in his teens and his university years. Almost the entire third chapter is devoted to the three-day religious retreat in Belvedere, where the hellfire and brimstone sermons of James Aloysius Cullen (named Father Arnall in the book) brought about Joyce's confession and religious redemption after his experience with a prostitute.

Throughout the narrative Stephen, like Dedalus and Icarus, soars upwards from the labyrinth to experience ecstatic moments of self-realization, only to fall to the ground again. His rejection of the priesthood in chapter four, for instance, is followed by a mystical encounter with a 'bird-like' girl in the moonlight on the beach at Bull Island, just north of Dublin, and the understanding that his future is 'to live, to err, to fall, to triumph, to recreate life out of life'. Yet by the next morning, as chapter five begins, the light-suffused watery pools on the island have been reduced to the 'yellow dripping' into which he dips his fried bread at breakfast. In the final long chapter of the book Stephen, who has been expected throughout his life, by his family, the Church and his teachers, to apologize and repent, makes his own statement of self-belief to his friend Cranly: 'I do not fear to be alone or to be spurned for another or to leave whatever I have to leave. And I am not afraid to make a mistake.' The last part of the novel is written as a diary to indicate that Stephen has now released himself from the labyrinth; he is viewing the forces that have moulded his life objectively rather than subjectively. As the 'portrait' ends Stephen is leaving Dublin, going 'to encounter for the millionth time the reality of experience and to forge in the smithy of my soul the uncreated conscience of my race.'

The completion of *Portrait* and its acceptance by a progressive literary circle released Joyce's mind to consider other projects. He began some preliminary work on a huge novel that he had long been contemplating, but put it to one side when he decided to write a play that he called 'Exiles'. Once again a work with an Irish setting, this draws on his fear of being cuckolded by Nora, and weaves together the strands from a number of incidents in their lives together. The chief characters of the play, Richard and Bertha Rowan, return to Dublin after a nine-year exile. A journalist friend named Robert Hand, loosely based on Gogarty and Cosgrave, attempts to take Bertha away from her husband. She tells Richard that Hand has kissed her, and now wishes her to meet him at a cottage outside Dublin. Richard tells her that he will not prevent the meeting, but goes to the cottage ahead of his wife to tell Robert he has decided to leave the couple together. The second Act ends with Robert and Bertha alone together in front of the bedroom door. The third Act offers no resolution of what happened between Robert and Bertha. Instead the reader is left wondering whether or not Bertha and Robert are lovers, an echo of Joyce's own doubts about Nora's relations with Cosgrave and Prezioso. 'Exiles' was not published until 1918. To a biographer its main interest is the extent to which the characters and situation of Richard and Bertha Rowan are based on those of Joyce and Nora. Some of the dialogue has the ring of genuine conversations between the couple, and its plot reflects Joyce's recurring suspicions about his wife. Although he was a lifelong enthusiast for the theatre, Joyce's one play does not suggest strong dramatic talent. 'Exiles' has been seen by critics as the least satisfactory of his major works, and its debt to Ibsen's 'When We Dead Awaken' has often been pointed out. Yet the influence of Joyce's novels, with their interior monologue technique, on modern writing for the theatre has been very great.

In July 1914 the assassination of the Archduke Ferdinand in Sarajevo, a few hundred miles south of Trieste, precipitated the First World War. Joyce had a low opinion of all governments and wanted nothing to do with the conflict. As he remarked to Francini: 'My political faith can be expressed in a word. Monarchies, constitutional or unconstitutional, disgust me. Kings are mountebanks. Republics are slippers for everyone's feet. Temporal power is gone and good riddance.' He was happy to stay in apparent safety in Trieste with his family, with little more to disturb him than the problems of getting his instalments of *Portrait* over to the *Egoist* in London. But in January 1915 Stanislaus Joyce was arrested and placed in an internment camp. Unlike James he had involved himself closely with the Irredentist movement that sought to return his adopted city to Italy, and was considered a security risk by the Austrian authorities. He would not be released until 1918. The war, however, did precipitate one change in Joyce's domestic arrangements. In 1914 his sister Eileen had become engaged to a Czech bank official name Frantisek Schaurek, a good-hearted man who was a keen collector of antiques. With the advent of the war, and the uncertainty of her position as a foreign national, the couple decided to put forward their wedding, which took place in April 1914. When Eileen moved in with her husband, Nora and James found themselves living alone together with their children for almost the first time since 1904.

Early in 1915 Italy declared war on Austria, bringing Trieste into the forefront of the coming bitter campaign between the two countries. The Joyces, as foreign nationals who held passports from Great Britain, a hostile power, found themselves in a difficult situation. The Austrian authorities began weeding out unwanted foreigners and interning them. James went to the neutral American consul, who was looking after

British interests, and made his preparations to flee. In late June he, Nora and the children, having been granted exit papers from the Austrians, began the train journey to Zurich in neutral Switzerland. To their discomfort there was a long halt at Innsbruck, the last stop in Austrian territory, and they feared they might be arrested. But nothing happened and at the end of July 1915 they arrived safely in the Swiss city, to begin a second exile in Joyce's life. Apart from a short return after the war, the Trieste years were over, as were the long years of teaching. A new stage was about to begin, one that would be dominated by the writing of his masterpiece *Ulysses,* the most important novel of the twentieth century.

CHAPTER VI

Ulysses

Joyce found Zurich a very different city to the bustling, untidy Mediterranean port from he had just been ousted by the war. Surrounded by the white peaks of the Alps (in Joyce's opinion 'those great lumps of sugar'), its clean and ordered streets offered an austere contrast to those of untidy, happy-go-lucky Trieste. The city was German-speaking, leaving Nora and his children the unwelcome task of learning another language on top of the Italian they had learnt in Trieste. For the moment they had no choice but to stay in the neutral haven of Switzerland. The family settled into a room on Reinhardstrasse, the first of several they rented during the years they spent in the city, and schools were found for Giorgio and Lucia. As usual Joyce and Nora were broke, but a gift of £15 from Nora's uncle Michael tided them over their first weeks in Switzerland.

The war had turned Zurich into a crossroads, and it harboured artistic and cultural refugees from across Europe. Lenin, Jung and a dozen other leaders and thinkers who would make their mark on the century could be seen in its cafés, along with the young artists who were in the process of founding the Bauhaus modernist design movement. Writers staying in the city included Romain Rolland, Stephan Zweig and Franz

Wedekind, along with less well-known figures from a dozen different European countries. Joyce fitted comfortably into this cosmopolitan atmosphere, and could soon be seen drinking and conversing with other novelists and artists at the fashionable Café Voltaire, the Odeon or the Pfauen restaurant. He favoured white wines like Riesling, Fendant and Sion, and Chianti, and ended many a boisterous evening jigging or dancing to amuse his friends. Joyce, with his garrulous ways and keen Irish wit, quickly attracted a circle of new friends. The closest of these were Ottocaro Weiss, a student from Trieste who shared his interest in music, and Frank Budgen, an English artist who painted a fine portrait of Nora in 1918. Budgen, a convivial drinking partner, became the writer's sounding board for his ideas on *Ulysses,* and later wrote the book *James Joyce and the Making of Ulysses.* Joyce made other contacts through the language students he took on to help pay expenses. Thanks to his growing literary reputation, and the championing of W. B. Yeats and Ezra Pound, his financial burden was alleviated when he received the sum of £85 from the Royal Literary Fund in England. Another grant of £100 was obtained from the Civil List, again through the intercession of Yeats and Pound.

The uncompromising writer was beginning to achieve a measure of recognition, yet the difficulties in getting his work before the public continued. In 1915 and 1916 five English publishers rejected *Portrait*, largely because they feared that its explicit scenes and language might leave them open to obscenity charges. Joyce was despairing of the book ever appearing in hard covers when, in October 1916, he had a pleasant surprise. W. B. Huebsch, a young New York publisher who admired his work, wrote offering to publish American editions of both *Dubliners* and *Portrait*. He gave Joyce an advance of £54, which along with £50 he had already received from Harriet Weaver, represented the first profit he had made from any of his books. *A Portrait of the Artist as a Young Man* was published on 29 December 1916, a few weeks after the release of the American edition of *Dubliners*. The novel received mixed reviews from the critics, most of whom failed to comprehend the complex underlying structure that unified the narrative. Some were hostile. The reviewer of 'Everyman', for instance, thought 'Mr Joyce a clever novelist, but we feel he would be really at his best in a treatise on cleaning out drains.' H. G. Wells, on the other hand, praised it in the *Nation* as 'this most remarkable novel', whilst the *Times Literary Supplement* thought it 'full of wild music'. The publication of *Portrait* was encouraged by Harriet Shaw Weaver, Helen Marsden's successor as editor of the *Egoist*, who agreed to take 750 copies of the American edition for the English market. These were sold out within a few months, an indication that Joyce's fame was begin to spread beyond a handful of admirers. Harriet Weaver was to be Joyce's great patron over the coming years, and her financial gifts allowed Joyce to work on his writing without the crippling financial worries of his earlier years. The daughter of an English doctor, she had distanced herself from her wealthy family to pursue her interest in the feminist movement, Communism and avant-garde literature. A quiet, almost shy, woman who dressed in a style that was decades out of date and who cultivated an image of almost Victorian respectability, she was amongst the first to recognize Joyce's genius.

Following the completion of 'Exiles' in 1914 Joyce was ready to turn his mind to the huge new novel that he had already done some work on, and that had its origins in a short story he conceived in 1906 for *Dubliners* but did not write. In 1904, as related in an earlier chapter, one Alfred Hunter helped Joyce after he was hurt in a fight. The unwritten story compared the Jewish man and his unfaithful wife to the Greek hero Ulysses, who wandered for ten years after the fall of Troy, before returning home to his faithful consort Penelope. Joyce put the idea for his story away for almost eight years, but revived it when he had finished *Portrait*. Textual evidence from *Ulysses*, along with letters from this time, suggest that Joyce's original plan was to write a sequel to the newly finished novel, one that would possibly end with the death of his mother, although including some key events in his life that happened afterwards. The first book of *Ulysses*, which deals with Stephen Dedalus, appears to have been a re-writing of existing material for this novel, and utilizes Joyce's experiences in the Martello Tower with Gogarty, his brief teaching career, and his memories of walks on Sandymount Strand.

This 'proto-*Ulysses*' (as the scholar H. W. Gabler described it) evolved into the idea of having the novel take place within a single day in Dublin. In his revised scheme for the plot, each incident would correspond to one of the adventures of Homer's *Odyssey*. It was at this point, perhaps, that the author settled on basing his main characters on Hunter and his wife. Joyce's identification with Jews as outcasts and wanderers suggested Hunter as a modern parallel to the wandering Greek hero. He conceived his Everyman in Leopold Bloom, a Jewish Dubliner who works as an advertisement canvasser, and who is an amalgamation of Hunter, his Trieste friend Italo Svevo, and a dozen other men. Bloom's wife would be Molly, with an inner voice that belongs mainly to Nora, but with a face and body borrowed from the exotic beauties Joyce remembered from Trieste – like Amanda Popper and Signora Santos, the wife of a fruit-importer. Joyce constructed a background for Molly that placed her birth in Gibraltar, thus explaining away her dusky un-Irish appearance. Her words and thoughts in the famous inner monologue that ends *Ulysses,* however, would owe far more to Galway than to Spain.

In his vast new novel Joyce reinvented the way that novels were written. It was almost a series of experiments with words and ideas, each section trying to relate its everyday events by using revolutionary literary techniques. The most notable was the 'stream of consciousness', a way of writing which he did not invent (his model was an obscure French writer, Edouard Dujardin), but which he perfected. Novelists, before Joyce's time, could address their readers from three perspectives. They could write in the third person, relating their tales objectively from a 'God's eye' perspective, alternatively they could write subjectively in the first person, transmitting the story through the eyes and mind of the narrating character. A third method, which could be used to transcend the limits of the first or third persons, was to present the fiction in the form of journal entries or as a series of letters written by one or more of the novel's characters. This gave the fiction a more realistic feeling, but still did not correspond to the way the human mind actually thinks and experiences the world. In the 'stream of consciousness' Joyce set out to reproduce the way the human consciousness really perceives experience – in a constant flow of images, random ideas and memories. The stream of consciousness bears a certain resemblance to Freud's 'unconscious', although Joyce might have argued that his technique revealed the unspoken elements of the individual's awareness rather than the hidden. His interest was in the 'mystery of consciousness' rather than the 'mystery of the unconscious'.

The writing of *Ulysses* was a complex process, and required the most intense concentration from its author. Yet his day-to-day existence continued in the same irregular fashion as ever. The family lived in a series of small flats whilst in Zurich. For all of 1916 they lived in a damp apartment at 54, Seefeldstrasse, with a kitchen, living room and two small bedrooms. In this confined space he wrote the first version of Part I: 'Telemachus', 'Proteus' and 'Nestor'; and some of the later sections of the book involving Stephen Dedalus, working mainly from existing material and notes. In the daytime he spent a few hours teaching, then continued to work on the novel. At night Joyce went to meet his artist and writer friends, or took Nora to the theatre, partaking in the rich cultural life that Zurich offered during this period. In January 1917 the family moved again, to a flat with two large rooms at 73, Seefeldstrasse. They had only been in residence for a few weeks when Joyce was stricken by a blinding pain in his eyes while walking down the street. He was diagnosed as suffering from the retinal diseases synecchia and glaucoma, which can lead to blindness. He spent several months recovering, and could do little work on the book. He was beginning to recover when he caught tonsillitis, and had to spend another month in bed. His doctors blamed his health problems in part on Zurich's damp climate, and recommended he should go to recuperate in one of the milder parts of the country.

On 17 February 1917 a letter from a London firm of solicitors arrived, informing the ailing author that an anonymous admirer had donated him the gift of £200, to be paid in £50 stipends at three-monthly intervals. James and Nora were overjoyed by this completely unexpected gift, which at a stroke removed any money problems for many months to come, but were perplexed as to its source. It was several years later that they discovered their benefactor was Harriet Weaver, who had decided to support the writer from her large inheritance. Joyce's financial situation was further improved in March when John Quinn, an Irish-American lawyer with literary tastes, and a book collector, bought the manuscript of 'Exiles'. Joyce had been trying to have the play staged for some time, but with little success. When his first attempts to have the play staged in America failed, he approached the Abbey theatre in Dublin, but W. B. Yeats, despite hs sympathetic interest in Joyce, rejected it on the grounds that it did not fit into the self-consciously 'national' type of drama his Irish Literary Theatre was engaged in. He was no more successful in England, where the Stage Society were initially interested in producing it. The play was rejected by their Committee after some members became uneasy over its 'dirty' scenes; it would be 1926 before 'Exiles' was given its London première. Joyce's contract for *Dubliners* contained a clause dictating that Grant Richards must be offered 'Exiles' for publication first. The London publisher, as was his habit, hemmed and hawed for months before finally accepting the piece, which he published on 25 May 1918.

In August 1918 Nora, and the children departed for Locarno, in the warmer Italian-speaking part of Switzerland. Joyce was to follow a few days later, but before he could leave, his eye problems returned with a vengeance. He was again tormented by pain, and his ophthalmist had no choice but to perform an iridectomy on his damaged right eye. The operation was a success, but the writer was left with severely reduced vision in that eye. When Joyce finally reached Locarno the city disappointed him. He had toyed with the idea of settling there, but after a few weeks found its provincial atmosphere uncongenial after Zurich. The high point of his stay was an attempt to woo Gertrude Kaempffer, a twenty-six-year-old Prussian woman who was in the city recovering from tuberculosis. It was a rather mild flirtation, since Miss Kaempffer had no intention of pursuing a romance with a married man. Joyce did however send her the extraordinary letter, which she tore up, describing his first sexual experience

In January 1918 the Joyces abandoned Locarno to return to Zurich, where they took a new flat at 38 Universitätstrasse. Joyce's eye problems had restricted his ability to work during 1917 but the Locarno interlude saw the completion of the 'Telamachia' – the first part of *Ulysses* dealing with the movements of Stephen Dedalus between 8am and 11am. He sent it to Claude Sykes, a close friend who had agreed to type the manuscript if Joyce could find him a typewriter. This was obtained with the help of Rudolph Goldschmitt, another friend and language pupil, and by the end of December the manuscript was ready for posting off. Joyce, as always eager to bring in more money to cover his prodigious spending, wished to have the book serialized, and Harriet Weaver bought the English publication rights for the *Egoist*. In America, with the help of Ezra Pound, he came to an agreement with the *Little Review*, an American avant-garde periodical run by Margaret Anderson and Jane Heap. The two women, recognizing the importance of Joyce's work, were courageously prepared to face the inevitable problem of censorship, and began the serialization in the March 1918 issue of the magazine.

The Joyces were now as well off as they had ever been, although they rapidly spent any money they received with careless abandon. In early 1918 Joyce was given a further unexpected boost to his finances. Mrs Harold Roosevelt McCormick, a rich American expatriate, began paying the author 1,000 Swiss francs a month. Mrs McCormick was a well-known patroness of the arts in Zurich, and closely associated with Carl Jung, the great Swiss psychoanalyst. The stipend was handed over regularly until October 1918, when his benefactress unexpectedly instructed her solicitors to cease the payments. The most likely explanation for the decision is that Mrs McCormick was angry with Joyce because he refused to let himself be analysed by Jung. In a typically paranoid reaction, however, Joyce looked around for a betrayer, and settled on Ottocaro Weiss, who suddenly found himself frozen out by his former friend. Joyce's resentment may have been fuelled by the suspicion that Weiss was in love with Nora, and his fear that they might be deceiving him. The monthly payments, regardless of the circumstances surrounding their ending, had taken the financial pressure off Joyce during a very important part of the creation of *Ulysses*. On Mrs McCormick's death in 1933 he acknowledged 'her act prompted by kindness and generosity'.

Joyce had never lost his love for the theatre, and in the spring of 1918 he allowed himself to be persuaded by Claude Sykes to become involved in setting up 'The English Players', an amateur acting company that would present English language plays in Zurich. On 29 April 1918 the English players performed Oscar Wilde's 'The Importance of Being Earnest' at a Zurich theatre to a large and enthusiastic audience, ensuring that Joyce and Sykes would make a reasonable profit. The production, however, was marred by an unlooked-for quarrel. One of the men involved was Henry Carr, an official at the British Consulate in Zurich, who played the rakish Algernon Moncrieffe. Carr, a keen amateur actor, spent 150 francs on buying himself a new outfit so he could impress in his part. He was annoyed to receive only 10 francs expense money from the show, especially when he knew the company's managers had pocketed a quite sizable amount of profit. In retaliation he refused to give Joyce a sum of 25 francs he had obtained by selling tickets. A feud broke out between the two men, and Joyce took his case to Percy Bennett, the Consul-General in Zurich, and then to Sir Horace Rumbold, the British Ambassador in Berne. Neither would support the claim, and instead responded by writing a letter demanding that the half-blind writer volunteer for military service. Eventually Joyce took the offending actor to court, and was awarded the 25 francs plus 60 more in damages. In *Ulysses* he took further revenge on his enemies in the Zurich consulate, making Carr one of the gang of drunken English soldiers who knock down Stephen Dedalus, and Bennett his Sergeant Major.

In June the English players staged another performance. Joyce's hope was that they would produce 'Exiles', but instead three popular one-act plays were chosen – J.M. Barrie's 'The Twelve-Pound Look', Bernard Shaw's 'The Dark Lady of the Sonnets' and J. M. Synge's 'Riders to the Sea'. In the last play, which Joyce had first read in 1903 when he met its author in Paris, Nora took the minor role of Catheleen, the oldest daughter of the household. She had never acted before, but her strong Galway accent and majestic appearance turned Synge's Aran Islands tragedy into the evening's greatest success. Joyce continued his involvement with the group, whose productions included Shaw's 'Mrs Warren's Profession' (then banned in England) in its autumn programme. But his bad relations with the British Consulate had led to its staff boycotting the English Players, and towards the end of 1918 he left the company. 'Exiles' was first performed in August 1919, when a German translation was staged in Munich. To Joyce's disappointment the play flopped, and was dismissed by one newspaper reviewer as 'Irish stew'.

Ulysses was gathering bulk and from early 1918, when Joyce settled on the pattern of the book and decided to make Leopold Bloom its central character, the episodes flowed rapidly from his pen. The first four episodes of Part II: 'Calypso', 'Lotus Eaters', 'Hades', and 'Aeolus', were completed by August 1918. Between that date and his departure from Zurich in late 1919 Joyce completed a further five episodes, 'Lestrygonians', 'Scylla and Charybdis', 'Wandering Rocks', 'Sirens' and 'Cyclops'; and had began 'Nausicaa', the thirteenth episode of the novel. For all but one or two of these episodes Joyce's reference material, beyond his own memory and imagination, was not excessive. He had a copy of Homer's *Odyssey* to remind him of the details of each episode. This was supplemented by geographical notes suggesting the Mediterranean locations of each episode, based on the claims of the scholar Victor Bérard that the places visited by Ulysses were derived from Phoenician records. For his Dublin locations and background, Joyce used *Thom's Dublin Directory*, a useful reference for streets, businesses and other minutiae of commercial Dublin in the period. One very useful personal record was the so-called 'Alphabetical Notebook', composed by Joyce after returning to Trieste from his visit to Dublin in 1909. This list of sketches of family friends and other acquaintances provided a valuable source for the minor characters of the book. Joyce's other references included information on furniture and interior design in 1904 (culled from newspapers of the time), and notes on Dublin colloquialisms and contemporary slang.

To provide a framework for the novel Joyce had created a list of correspondences to run through the text. The 'schema', as it is called, links a 'scene', an hour, an organ of the body, an art, a colour, a symbol and a 'technic' to each of the incidents he took from Homer's epic. The increasing complexity of the work, and its experimental nature, began worrying even his closest supporters. Ezra Pound and Harriet Weaver were taken aback in May 1919 when they received 'The Sirens' episode from Joyce. In this famous adventure from Homer's epic, his hero has himself tied to the mast of his ship, to enable him to hear the song of the Sirens – spirits in the form of maidens whose singing lures passing mariners to their destruction. In Joyce's novel the scene is a Concert Room, the hour four o'clock in the afternoon. As the symbol for the sirens, Joyce chose the barmaids working in a bar (their Isle) next door to the Concert Hall. The organ is the ear, and the art music. No colour is allotted to this part of the novel. Joyce's technic is *fuga per canonem* (a musical term), and he mimics the sound of a musical performance throughout the section. The first two pages of 'The Sirens' is a mixed up jumble of onomatopoeic words and phrases that represents the orchestra tuning up, and ends with the conductors 'done' and 'begin' as the performance is ready to start. The text is dominated by musical terms and sound effects. The trills of the arpeggios, for example, are represented by words with their vowels left out. Bloom, in the bar, hears Stephen singing an aria from the opera 'Martha', the siren's song that makes him think of his wife Molly, whom he knows is about to meet her lover Blazes Boylan. As he listens to the song, he loops an elastic band around his fingers, the symbolic equivalent of the ropes that bind Ulysses to his mast. 'The Sirens' ends with Bloom pretending to look in a shop window, waiting for a tram to pass so he can fart:

> 'Tram. Kran, kran' kran. Good oppor. Coming.
> Krandlkrankran. I'm sure it's the burgundd. Yes.
> One, two. Let my epitaph be Kraaaaa. Written.
> I have.
> PPprrpffrrppfff.
> Done.'

Uneasy as they were with the content and revolutionary approach to language of the 'Sirens' episode (Pound wrote 'a new style per chapter not required'), his English and American patrons continued to provide invaluable encouragement and support.

In May 1919 Joyce was visiting Locarno with his artist friend and drinking companion Frank Budgen when he received wonderful news from Nora in Zurich. Another letter from the solicitors in London had arrived, informing him that his anonymous benefactor was about to settle £5,000 in War Bonds on him, which would pay £250 per annum. This largesse meant that he would have a permanent income to support his writing. The gift, although he did not guess it, was from Harriet Weaver. She had been in constant correspondence with the writer over the episodes in *Ulysses*, and had decided he must have security to allow him to give all his energies to his masterpiece. The form of the gift, which could not be cashed in, was probably the idea of her solicitor, who correctly guessed that the spendthrift Joyce was likely to fritter away any lump sum sent to him.

The year 1919 was marked by the most intense of Joyce's extra-marital 'romances'. It had its origins late in the previous year, when Joyce looked out of his flat at 29, Universitätstrasse and noticed an attractive young woman through the window of the building next door. She had just been to the toilet, and was pulling the chain. A few days later he saw her again on the street and followed her home. As the girl turned to go into her building he noticed she was limping. Then Joyce saw her face, and to his surprise it seemed to resemble the beautiful young woman he had seen, in an epiphanic moment, wading in the Irish Sea in his last year at Belvedere. Joyce was smitten. He wrote to the woman, whose name was Marthe Fleischmann, and began a secret correspondence with her. Miss Fleischmann, the mistress of an engineer named Hiltpold, was quite happy to indulge the writer's interest, although she put limits on any sexual involvement. The 'affair' climaxed in a dinner at Frank Budgen's studio on his birthday in 1919, which also happened to be Candlemas. Miss Fleischmann was Jewish, and her shy 'lover' borrowed an ornate candlestick from a friend, and a Chanukah candle to light for her. What happened next is uncertain, but it has been suggested that she allowed some sexual intimacy but not full intercourse. Joyce and Marthe Fleischmann exchanged letters for several months afterwards, although they did not meet again. In *Ulysses* his passion for the Swiss woman may have suggested the encounter in the 'Nausicaa' episode with Gertie MacDowell (in which she is 'fingered only'), and Bloom's love affair by mail with Martha Clifford. Eventually the young woman's indiscretion caused her to suffer a nervous collapse, which she blamed on her guilt at flirting with the Irishman. She confessed all to Hiltpold, and Joyce had to exert all his powers of diplomacy to soothe the feelings of the ruffled engineer.

With the end of the First World War in 1918 the Joyce family were free to return to Trieste if they wished. James and Nora had never been altogether happy in Zurich, and as the winter of 1919 approached they thought of returning to their adopted city, which had now been annexed by Italy. Stanislaus, following his release from the internment camp, was living in Trieste, as were Eileen and her husband; she now had two children who had yet to meet their uncle. The unexpected cancellation of Mrs McCormick's monthly allowance sealed Joyce's dissatisfaction with Zurich, and in October he and his family packed their possessions and moved back to Trieste. Joyce had arrived in Switzerland four years previously as a penniless language teacher with unfulfilled literary aspirations. He was leaving with a growing reputation as one of the leading avant-garde writers in Europe. As yet his reputation was limited, but the next decade would see him established as the most discussed writer in the English language.

CHAPTER VII

*P*ARIS AND PUBLICATION

The return of James and Nora to Trieste proved to be only a temporary interlude, rather than a renewal of their pre-war life in the city. Stanislaus did not welcome them with open arms when they moved into the flat he shared with Eva and her husband on the Via Sanita. During his internment Joyce's younger brother had realized he wanted to live his own life, free from the monetary and emotional demands of his elder brother. He was repelled by James's heavy drinking, and showed little interest in the complicated new novel he was writing. The bond between the two brothers, if not altogether severed, had been fatally weakened. Stanislaus had his own social circle and interests now, and was not prepared to be the prop that supported his brother's ever-tottering household. To Joyce, the provinciality of Trieste, now just another medium-sized Italian city rather than the maritime hub of the Austrian empire, was depressing after the heady intellectual atmosphere of Zurich. The years in Switzerland had widened the writer's cultural horizons, and he was unable to feel at ease in the small-town atmosphere of the Mediterranean port. Joyce began thinking of leaving Italy, and settled on London as his new destination. At least part of his reason for choosing England was to be nearer his father. John

Joyce had not changed in any way, but James still felt some fondness for the old man, with whom he remained in contact. London was only twenty-fours away from Dublin by boat and train and would allow John Joyce to visit him regularly.

Joyce's dissatisfaction with Trieste hampered his efforts to write. Now that Stanislaus was not interested in in his literary plans there was nobody for him to bounce his ideas off. Joyce lost heart and for some months seriously considered abandoning *Ulysses.* Fortunately he was still corresponding regularly with his Zurich confidant Frank Budgen, who encouraged him not to give up. With a supreme effort of will the Irishman returned to his troublesome task. He finished the 'Nausicaa' episode, and then began composing 'The Oxen of the Sun', perhaps the most difficult section of the entire work for the ordinary reader to comprehend. The chapter takes place in a lying-in hospital, where a character named Mrs Purefoy is giving birth. In it Joyce paralleled the nine stages of the embryonic development of a human child by writing the long episode in nine different styles. Each represents a stage in the evolution of literary English, beginning with Anglo-Saxon and passing through the medieval, Elizabethan, Jacobean and Georgian eras, until it culminates in the modern age, represented by a hubbub of pidgin words, slang and regional dialects. Joyce was in the throes of this ambitious experiment when a meeting with Ezra Pound, in June 1919, led him to move to a more congenial city than the socially and culturally limited Trieste.

Despite their long correspondence, this was the first meeting between the two men. Pound was aware of Joyce's unhappiness, and arranged to see him in Sirmione, a resort on

Lake Garda in northern Italy, so that they could discuss his future plans. When Joyce finally arrived, after a delay caused by a train accident that prevented his departure from Trieste, Pound suggested the Irishman should move to Paris. In those post-war years the French capital was the heart of the Modernist movement, and home to its greatest writers and artists. Pound offered to prepare the way for Joyce by introducing his works to his friends in the city. Believing Joyce to be destitute, he had even brought along a second-hand suit and shoes for the impoverished writer to wear when he got there. The American poet was favourably impressed with the Irishman. 'Joyce – pleasing,' he wrote to John Quinn afterwards, 'after the first shell of cantankerous Irishman, I got the impression that the real man is the author of *Chamber Music*, the sensitive. The rest is genius.' During their conversation Pound and Joyce tried to work out who the Irish writer's unknown benefactor might be. After much debate they decided it was possibly Lady Cunard, an extremely rich patroness of the arts. But a few weeks later Joyce received a letter from Harriet Weaver, finally disclosing herself as the person who had been anonymously giving him money. Now that her generosity was in the open she became Joyce's 'fairy godmother', and continued to support him financially whilst he was finishing *Ulysses* and writing *Finnegans Wake*.

Around this time Joyce's perennial financial problems forced him to agree to sell the manuscript of *Ulysses* to John Quinn. In June 1920 he sent the first batch of episodes off to the United States, and from then onwards to the completion of the book in 1922, he dispatched the handwritten chapters when they were finished and typed up. In all Quinn paid him

$1,200 for the manuscript, plus another $240 when he sold the manuscript on to Dr A.S.W. Rorsenbach in 1923. Although the American collector treated him fairly, and gave him half of his profit from the deal with Rorsenbach, Joyce considered he had been cheated. He made a scene and declared he wanted to buy the manuscript back, but in the end his threats came to nothing. The hand-written manuscript of *Ulysses* is now in the collection of the Rorsenbach Foundation in Philadelphia, but there are questions as to whether some of its chapters include all of Joyce's final corrections and changes. He was an inveterate tinkerer with his work, and often added or omitted words and sentences on the typescripts and proofs of his books before publishing them. It has also been suggested that Joyce bamboozled Quinn by recopying some of the passages in the Rorsenbach manuscript, either from his original texts or from corrected typewritten copies and the printer's proofs. If Joyce did this, his motive was to provide clearer pages than his scribbled-over revisions, since Quinn indicated when buying the manuscript that a neat appearance would lead to a much higher price. Regardless of Joyce's motives, it was inevitable (given his declining eyesight) that he would make mistakes when he re-copied the pages. The inconsistencies between the Rorsenbach manuscript and the original 1922 Shakespeare and Company edition of *Ulysses* have caused great problems for scholars trying to settle on an accurate version of Joyce's text. This has been exacerbated by the fact that the novel was set by French typesetters, who were unfamiliar with English spelling and punctuation (not that that would have necessarily made much difference with large sections of the novel).

In July 1920 Joyce and Nora left Trieste for good. The departure marked the final breakdown of his intimacy with Stanislaus, his prop and helper during the early struggles to become a writer in Dublin and Trieste. Although they wrote to each other and met on three occasions afterwards, Joyce later said of this parting: 'The relations between the two brothers practically end here.' It is hard not to feel sympathy for Stanislaus, who received little thanks from James or Nora for his sacrifices on their behalf. His contribution was ignored even in *Portrait*, where Joyce diminished the role of the faithful younger brother so Stephen could stand in heroic artistic isolation. Stanislaus married in 1927, and made an academic career in his adopted city, later becoming an invaluable source of information for Joyce's principal biographer Richard Ellman. But his opinions were coloured by his simmering resentment against his brother, who he felt had treated him badly in Trieste and ignored him in his writings. In part this was a result of his own character, which lacked the reckless streak that his brother had inherited from John Joyce. 'I have never dared to act as I please,' Stanislaus wrote in his autobiographical *The Dublin Diary* (1962), 'but think in a little way "what will be thought of it?"'

James Joyce arrived in Paris on 8 July 1920, intending to spend a week or so in the city before leaving for London. He and Nora stayed there for twenty years, apart from numerous holidays and a few months in 1931 when they moved to England. On their arrival in Paris the family were broke and homeless, but Ezra Pound found free lodgings in a small flat belonging to a friend. The American writer, honouring the promise he made in Sirmione, introduced his *protégé* around the city's thriving artistic and cultural community. Amongst the various literary people that Joyce met during his first weeks in Paris was an American expatriate called Sylvia Beach, who owned a small English language bookshop, Shakespeare and Company, at that time in the Rue Dupuytren. Both she and her lesbian partner Adrienne Monnier, the owner of another bookshop, were well known in the city's literary circles. Miss Beach was already familiar with Joyce's earlier works, and became one of his most useful supporters in Paris. Joyce, now that he was living in the cultural centre of Europe rather than the backwater of distant Trieste, attracted visits from a number of writers who were aware of his growing reputation. The poet T. S. Eliot, accompanied by the artist and novelist Wyndham Lewis, arrived from London with a parcel from Ezra Pound, which proved to be a pair of old brown shoes. They found Joyce pleasant enough, although he impressed them as arrogant and dismissive of his literary contemporaries. They were surprised when the supposedly hard-up Irish genius took them to dinner, and on leaving gave the waiter a huge tip. Thanks to Harriet Weaver, who had just given him another £2,000, the 'destitute' writer was once again in funds.

Ulysses was nearing completion, although the novel progressed frustratingly slowly and was taking longer to write than he expected. By the end of January 1921, however, Joyce had reached the end of the controversial 'Circe' episode. This chapter, in which Leopold Bloom visits a brothel, takes place at midnight, and is notable for its orgiastic and hallucinatory descriptions. It concludes the second part of the novel, and contains some of the most sexually explicit and bizarre passages in the work. Joyce used his old memories of the Monto to describe Mrs Cohen's brothel and its inhabitants, but its fantastical orgy scenes (which culminate in Bloom turning into a woman) parodied Leopold von Sacher-Masoch's erotic novel *Venus in Furs*. Following this key chapter, which establishes Bloom and Dedalus as father-son figures, Joyce approached the third and last part of the novel – the *Nostos* or 'Homecoming'. Its three chapters correspond to Ulysses' return to his kingdom of Ithaca, and his defeat of Penelope's suitors. Joyce began 'Eumaeus', the first chapter of Part III in February 1921, but it was September before he was ready to tackle 'Ithaca', the next. Here Bloom returns to his house at 7, Eccles Street, accompanied by Stephen Dedalus, who has been knocked down by some drunken British soldiers. 'Ithaca' ends with the Jewish journalist safely curled up in bed with his wife; like Joyce himself and Nora, they sleep upside down to each other, with Bloom's head resting on Molly's feet.

As a narrative this chapter, which concludes with a large full stop, ends the day of Joyce's Everyman. Yet Joyce incorporated one final episode, arguably the most memorable in the whole book. 'Penelope', the last chapter of *Ulysses,* is thirty-six pages long and divided into a mere eight sentences. It is a 'stream of consciousness' interior monologue, in which Molly Bloom lies musing in bed beside her husband. Her thoughts ramble erratically over the day's events, her youthful memories of Gibraltar, her lovers and her husband. The novel concludes with Molly recalling her first sexual encounter with Bloom on the Hill of Howth, some sixteen years previously; '… and first I put my arms around him yes and drew him down to me so he could feel my breasts all perfume yes and his heart was going like mad and yes I said yes I will Yes.' In this chapter Joyce recreated Gibraltar with the same immaculate detail as he described Dublin; readers of the novel who knew the colony were amazed he had never been there. Molly's childhood memories of Gibraltar, nonetheless, share much with Nora's of Galway. Bloom's wife may be represented as a sultry woman of the Mediterranean, but her inner voice belongs to Joyce's wife alone. Molly may complain about her weak and foolish husband, but her interior monologue culminates with the reaffirmation of her love for him. Like Penelope in Homer's epic, and Nora in Trieste and Zurich, she values the emotional ties of marriages more than the temporary refuge of a casual affair.

Joyce was writing the 'Penelope' episode when the long running campaign to ban the novel in the United States, because of its alleged obscenity, began. In retrospect it seems absurd that any of _Ulysses_ could be considered pornographic or morally harmful, but there was a strong puritanical movement to 'cleanse' American society in the aftermath of the First World War. In 1919 the US Post Office commenced the campaign against Joyce by confiscating issues of the _Little Review_ with extracts from _Ulysses_, on the grounds they contained strong language or sexually explicit passages. In the course of twelve months the postal authorities intercepted and burnt the copies of the periodical containing 'Lestrygonians', 'Scylla and Charabydis' and 'Cyclops'. The attempts to suppress the book escalated in July 1920, when the _Little Review_ published the 'Nausicaa' episode, in which Bloom is sexually aroused at the sight of Gertie MacDowell's knickers. John Sumner of the powerful New York Society for the Prevention of Vice lodged a complaint, and the magazine's editors, Jane Heap and Margaret Anderson, were arrested on charges of publishing obscene material. At their trial, which began on 14 February 1921, the accused publishers were represented by John Quinn, an attorney by profession. Several expert witnesses defended 'Nausicaa' against the accusation that it was indecent, but the three judges trying the case refused to accept their opinions. They fined the defendants $50 each, and banned them from publishing any further extracts from the book.

Sumner's victory against the editors of the *Little Review* was disastrous to any future hopes of seeing *Ulysses* published in the United States. B. W. Huebsch, the American publisher of *Dubliners* and *Portrait of the Artist* reluctantly declined the new novel as a result of the verdict, and no other publishing house was prepared to risk prosecution by taking on the book on. By April 1921 Joyce was close to despair; he feared that his masterpiece might not be able to find a publisher. Then Sylvia Beach came forward, and offered to publish the book for him under the imprint of her Paris bookshop, Shakespeare and Company. She proposed a limited first edition of 1,000 copies, which she would try to subscribe in advance, with the author receiving a very generous two-thirds of any profits. The printing would include 100 signed copies on expensive Holland paper, to be retailed at 350 francs, 150 deluxe copies (*verge d'arches* paper) to sell at 250 francs each, and the remaining 750 copies to sell as a standard edition (linen paper) at 150 francs. Harriet Weaver assisted Sylvia Beach by passing on her customer lists, and agreed to publish an Egoist Press edition of 2,000 copies for the English market.

It took some months to prepare the manuscript for publication, since it had to be typed up, then proofed and re-proofed by the author; as always he made many revisions and corrections in his text. This time-consuming process did not pass without problems, and there was a near-disaster when the husband of a typist who was transcribing the manuscript casually picked it up one day. When he read the contents he was so offended that he threw some of the pages into the fire. Fortunately his wife was able to rescue most of them afterwards, and the book's author reconstructed the missing portions from earlier drafts and his notes. Joyce's eyesight was still causing him many problems, and hindered his reading of the typescripts and proofs, but he wore himself out trying to have the book ready for the printers on schedule. The Irishman, with his superstitious concern for dates, had his heart set on publishing the book on his fortieth birthday in 1922.

In December 1921, Sylvia Beach arranged for the French writer and critic Valéry Larbaud to give a public lecture on Joyce at her bookshop. Two hundred and fifty people attended the event, which included readings of extracts from *Ulysses* in French. The complex task of translating Joyce's idiosyncratic English text was entrusted to Jacques Benoist-Michens, a brilliant student of Larbaud's, who was only nineteen at the time. Some Joycean scholars believe that Benoist-Michens inadvertently suggested the final 'Yes' with which the Irish writer ended the novel. The translator, unhappy with the grammar of the French version of Joyce's original ending, 'Yes I will', added 'oui' to Molly Bloom's interior monologue.

On 2 February 1922 Joyce received three copies of *Ulysses* – all that were ready on the official publication date – from its printer Maurice Daratière. He presented the first numbered copy of the print run to his patroness Harriet Weaver, (Number 1000 he gave to Nora). As the rest of the copies arrived during the following weeks they were sent off to their various subscribers. Although hampered by personal difficulties, eye disease, and the hostility of the American censors, Joyce had finally placed his epic book before the reading public. His novel about the events of one short day in the Dublin of his young manhood, had consumed seven years of his life. His great undertaking had been carried out in three different European cities, and at times he worked whilst in crushing financial difficulty or under great personal stress. Joyce had put all of his creative energies into the work and was now exhausted. It remained to be seen whether the long and difficult book would be received as a work of genius, or dismissed as the obscure and obscene ramblings of a literary eccentric.

The opinions of Joyce's contemporaries about *Ulysses* covered a wide spectrum. George Moore, the novelist insulted by Joyce in his youthful attacks on Irish writers, dismissed it as 'hopeless'. He commented that 'Joyce thinks because he prints all the dirty little words he is a great novelist'. W. B. Yeats, in contrast, subscribed to the book, and despite some misgivings about its avant-garde style, declared it 'a work perhaps of genius'. But he later confessed that he had been unable to finish it. Some of the most interesting comments came from George Bernard Shaw, who refused to subscribe to the novel on the grounds that it was too expensive. Shaw, having spent his early years in Dublin, recognized the accuracy of Joyce's description of Stephen Dedalus and his friends. 'It is a revolting record of a disgusting phase of civilization,' he wrote to Sylvia Beach, 'but it is a truthful one … to me it is all hideously real. I have walked those streets and known those shops and taken part in those conversations.' Other writers responded variously to Joyce's work, although in general the older generation was less impressed than his contemporaries. Gertrude Stein, the *doyenne* of the American literary scene in Paris, considered that 'Joyce has done something. His influence however is local. Like Synge, another Irish writer, he has had his day.' Ernest Hemingway, on the other hand thought 'Joyce has a most goddam wonderful book.' His fellow countrymen Scott Fitzgerald and T. S. Eliot thought equally highly of the Irishman's achievement.

Reviews of the book in the more serious literary reviews varied. Some damned Joyce with faint praise, but Arnold Bennett in the *Outlook* and John Middleton Murry in the *Nation* wrote favourably and stressed its unique importance. Yet censorship ensured that many years would pass before *Ulysses* was readily available in most of the English-speaking world. Although not on the banned list in Ireland, the book was not displayed openly until the 1970s, whilst the 1921 prosecution of the *Little Review* prevented its official publication in the United States. Harriet Weaver's edition of the novel, published under her Egoist Press imprint, eventually suffered a similar fate. Her 2,000 copies, bound from the same sheets as the Shakespeare and Company printing, were made available in October 1922, and sent from Paris to retail and private customers in Britain, as well as to a large number of American subscribers. By January 1923 400 of the copies posted to the USA had been intercepted and destroyed by the authorities there. Miss Weaver arranged to have a further 500 copies bound up to replace these. She then tried to bring them into England, but Customs officers at Folkestone impounded the shipment. The entire re-printing was lost, excepting only a few copies that had been posted directly to London. Following the Folkestone seizure *Ulysses* was officially banned in England.

Joyce sent copies of the finished book to his father and other close relatives. John Joyce, although pleased with his son's fame and literary success, did not like its contents. Stanislaus was also dubious about his brother's novel; whilst he admired the accurate reconstruction of Dublin, he felt great distaste for some of its episodes and language. Joyce's aunt Josephine Murray would not have the book in her house, and lent it out as soon as possible. Nora's refusal to read it continues to be one of the most widely known stories about her relationship with Joyce. Since she had shared her life with Joyce throughout its composition, she was already familiar with many of its scenes. Nora disliked the vulgarity of what she had seen and heard of the manuscript of the novel, and was possibly upset that her own most intimate experiences had been recycled into Molly's interior monologue. Another contributory factor was that – like thousands of its readers since – she found the novel difficult to follow. For whatever reason, she reacted to the gift of her numbered copy from Joyce by asking a bystander: 'How much will you give me for it?'

Yet Nora's lack of interest in the novel equally reflected her frustration with her domestic life and Joyce's attitude towards her. Nora had shared in his struggle to establish his literary reputation for almost twenty years before *Ulysses* made James Joyce a world famous name. She did not idolize her partner as did literary women like Harriet Weaver and Sylvia

Beach, and his rise to fame bemused her. Nora was grateful for their new wealth, but years of hardship had left her resentful. Joyce's eye problems were growing more and more serious, and were being exacerbated by his refusal to stop drinking. In the course of the year following the publication of *Ulysses* her simmering dissatisfaction with her husband boiled over into a serious quarrel that temporarily divided them.

The row was caused by Nora's desire to bring her children home to visit Galway; she may even have been considering staying there permanently. She was in her late thirties now, and going through her own personal crisis. Since her early twenties she had been living in her partner's shadow, and she was tired of his expectations of her. It was her long-standing wish to see her mother and sisters again, and perhaps show them how well the black sheep of the family had done in the years since her last visit. Joyce stubbornly refused to go back to Ireland, and was reluctant to let her and the children go without him. Following his unhappy experiences on his last trip, the irate writer had sworn never to return; Ireland might have a paramount place in his past, but he would allow it no place in his future. His paranoid fears that Dublin was crawling with his personal enemies, all conspiring to harm him, had not abated. Like his phobias about dogs and thunder, they were part of the fabric of his personality. Furthermore, Joyce believed his portrayal of Dublin and its citizens might make him a target for extreme nationalists: Ireland was currently engaged in warfare between the British army and its irregular supplementary cohorts, and the Irish republicans.

Until early 1922 Joyce could point to the guerrilla campaign against the British army as a strong reason for Nora to stay in France, but a few weeks before the launch of *Ulysses,* Britain ratified the treaty granting Irish independence. The official ending of hostilities between the British army and the IRA freed Nora to go to Ireland, and since Harriet Weaver had just given Joyce another £1,500, the money for the trip was amply available. Still he continued to drag his feet about the journey, and Nora finally lost her patience. She told him she was going whether he liked it or not, and left Paris with her children, threatening never to return. Joyce was frantic without his family, and came perilously close to a nervous breakdown. 'You don't understand how this is affecting me,' he told one friend. 'I am worried all of the day and it does my eye no good.' Much of his anxiety focused on the outbreak of civil war in Ireland, following the refusal of Eamon de Valera to accept the division of the island between the 'Free State' and Northern Ireland. His fears were not unfounded. After a short visit to John Joyce in Dublin, Nora and her two children went to see her mother in Galway. She found that the pro- and anti-Treaty forces in the city were turning it into an armed camp, and had only been there for a few days when fighting broke out. Nora fled Galway at once, but had a frightening experience when her train to Dublin was fired at. There were no casualties, but she returned to Paris without stopping in Dublin to see Josephine Murray and her daughters.

Joyce was relieved at the safe return of Nora, Giorgio and Lucia, but their misfortune copper-fastened his refusal to step foot on the shores of Ireland again. He convinced himself that the shooting-up of Nora's train was not accidental. The incident was the cement that completed the wall he had built between himself and his homeland. Nothing, not even the last chance to say goodbye to his dying father, could draw James Joyce back into the orbit of his imaginary enemies. But he remained saturated with his native country – an anti-Irish Irishman who simultaneously rejected and embraced her history, culture and folklore to create the multi-layered worlds of *Ulysses* and *Finnegans Wake*.

Joyce had neglected his health in his toils to finish and proof-read *Ulysses,* and he was too physically and mentally exhausted to consider a new work for some time. His damaged eyesight remained a major cause of concern to all around him. In the summer of 1922 he suffered another severe attack of iritis, and the doctors decided that he needed another major operation on his eyes. There were other ailments. His teeth needed to be extracted and remedial work was required on his arthritic back. Before undergoing these treatments Joyce wanted a holiday, so in August 1922 the family travelled to London. Here, Joyce met Harriet Weaver for the first time. His patroness had continued her unstinting support, even though many of Joyce's friends and acquaintances thought he was abusing her generosity. In 1921 the novelist Wyndham Lewis warned her about Joyce's heavy drinking and extravagance, and she was worried enough to write and voice her unhappiness about his 'excess'. Joyce replied with a long letter explaining and excusing himself: 'There is a curious honour code amongst men,' he wrote, 'which obliges them to assist one another and not hinder the free action of one another and remain together with the result that very often they waken up the next morning sitting in the same ditch.' Harriet Weaver, who had total belief in Joyce's importance to twentieth-century literature, accepted his self-justification and continued to provide her emotional and financial support.

Before meeting his patroness the Irishman decided he would not modify his behaviour. She would have to take him as he was. He made a point of tipping his taxicab driver lavishly in front of her, and ordered the best wines at their dinner. Nonetheless he and Miss Weaver got on well together. The austere Englishwoman accepted that genius had its rights, and never judged or censored Joyce, no matter how outrageous his requests for more money or favours. She asked for nothing in return except the privilege of helping a great writer create his masterpieces by releasing him from the toils of making his own living. Joyce's gratitude to her was totally sincere, and on a personal level he charmed Harriet Weaver with his old-fashioned formality and politeness. He returned to Paris confident that he could count on the help of his patroness whilst writing his next book. About a year later, after he had started work on *Finnegans Wake,* Harriet Weaver gave him £12,000, her largest gift yet. The income from this huge sum, the equivalent of around £600,000 in today's values, should have kept Joyce in comfort for the rest of his life. Yet within a few years he was depleting this capital, and by the time of his death his estate was worth less than £1,000.

Joyce's cousins Alice and Kathleen, the daughters of Josephine Murray, were living in London. Before leaving the city he took them out to dinner. Nora had offended his aunt Josephine by not visiting her in Ireland, and she was still angry with him. During the evening Joyce asked the girls whether their mother had enjoyed the copy of *Ulysses* he sent her. They informed him that Mrs Murray did not think the book was fit to read, and refused to have it in the house.

'If *Ulysses* is not fit to be read,' he replied, 'life isn't fit to be lived.'

Joyce's stay in England was cut short by further problems with his sight, and he hastened back to Paris to consult with his specialist Dr Borsch. He was still feeling restless and decided to winter on the Riviera, but once again his holiday was cut short because of ill health. Soon after his return he embroiled himself in two needless quarrels. The first was with Sylvia Beach and Adrienne Monnier. Since the publication of *Ulysses,* he had been harassing the two women to persuade their literary contacts to review the book. He now exasperated his publisher by demanding that she reprint the novel, even though it had been subscribed and issued as a limited edition. She responded with a sharp letter telling him she was not in the business of 'hustling' books. For good measure, she added that there were so many unpleasant rumours about *Ulysses* and its author that she thought it would be unwise to draw any further attention to either. Joyce pointed out that the Egoist Press copies of the book – which Sylvia Beach complained were almost identical to her own – could be clearly identified as a second edition. The argument finally fizzled out and normal relations were restored between them.

Joyce's second quarrel was a direct result of his paranoia, and caused a long rift with Frank Budgen, his mainstay from the years he was writing *Ulysses* in Zurich. The two remained close even after Joyce moved to France. In 1921, after receiving Harriet Weaver's complaints about his extravagance, the Irishman forwarded the letter to Budgen, and asked for advice on how to deal with her. But after Miss Weaver assured him of her continuing support, Joyce regretted showing the letter to the artist. He could simply have asked for it back, but he was incapable of trusting anybody, and instead resorted to a shoddy trick against his friend. The next time Budgen came to see him in Paris, he told him to bring the letter, because he needed to read it again. Joyce took the artist out on the town and plied him with drinks until he passed out. The writer then removed Budgen's wallet and extracted the compromising letter. The next morning Joyce returned the wallet, explaining that he had removed it for safekeeping. When Budgen found that Joyce had extracted the letter without a word to him, he was furious at the duplicity, and did not speak to him for three years.

Joyce, notwithstanding his recurring near-blindness and erratic state of mind after the publication of *Ulysses*, was beginning to turn his thoughts to a new book. In April 1923 he had his teeth removed, following which Borsch performed an operation called an sphincterectomy on the muscles of his eyelid. Shortly afterwards Joyce confided the title of his next book to Nora, and warned her not to tell anybody. He did not intend to reveal it to the world until shortly before its publication date; for years to come it was to be known to his readers only as 'Work in Progress'. Until 1938 only Joyce and Nora knew its real title was *Finnegans Wake,* after the well-known Irish–American drinking song about a Dublin labourer, Tim Finnegan, who is revived from the dead after whisky is accidentally poured on his corpse. It was to be an even more ambitious novel than its predecessor, a book of the night as *Ulysses* was a book of the day. Shortly afterwards Harriet Weaver asked Joyce what his next book would be about. He replied that it would be 'a universal history'. The seventeen years that it took to finish the book would consume the remainder of its author's creative life, years that would bring him personal tragedy and public success in equal measure.

CHAPTER VIII

A LIFE OF LUXURY

Joyce began sketching out the shape of *Finnegans Wake* in Bognor, a prim resort on England's south coast where he and his family were holidaying during the summer of 1923. The novel was originally planned as a loose sequel to *Ulysses*, but where that book had dealt with the day, his new work would deal with the sleeping hours. Instead of the inner world of conscious thought, *Finnegans Wake* would be set in the strange landscape of human dreams. Joyce's new book was not going to be easy to interpret, any more than the language and meaning of our sleeping thoughts are. 'They say it's obscure,' he was to reply to critics of *Finnegans Wake*. 'They compare it with *Ulysses*. But the action of *Ulysses* was chiefly in the daytime. The action of my new work takes place at night. It's natural things shouldn't be so clear at night, isn't it now.' This may have been so, but even enthusiastic supporters of his genius like Ezra Pound and Harriet Weaver were baffled by the first samples they read of the book. Joyce created a new language of his own to express the universal language of sleep, based on the Dublin dialect he had grown up hearing, but incorporating words from almost fifty languages. Much of *Finnegans Wake* is almost unreadable on the page, and at times seems like mere babble. Yet it is never meaningless, and the simplest key to understanding and enjoying the book is by reading it aloud rather than trying to follow it in the conventional way on the written page. Joyce deliberately chooses to express himself through the sound of his words and wordplay, just as in the darkness of night what we hear is more important than what we see. It was an extraordinary experiment, as revolutionary in literature as the paintings of the Cubists and Surrealists were in art. But few of his contemporaries could understand his intensely personal vision, and the extracts he later published from the 'Work in Progress' were to be dismissed by many critics as misguided or even a hoax.

In 1923, however, all this was before the Irishman. Whilst at Bognor he received news of Miss Weaver's munificent gift of £12,000. He wrote to thank her, stating that without her help his task would be almost impossible. He and Nora returned to Paris, revived after the turmoil of the previous two years, and began looking for a new flat. Although they had been living in the French capital for several years, they had yet to settle anywhere permanently, and had been camping in a series of hotels and friends' flats since their arrival in 1920. Once they had found a new home, Joyce began working on the new project in earnest, and threw himself into the round of daytime writing and night-time socializing that was his customary way of life. He was a celebrity in Paris now, and there were many inaccurate tales told about the 'mysterious' Irish writer. Joyce wrote to Harriet Weaver that he was variously believed to have been a spy, a cocaine addict, the owner of a chain of Swiss cinemas, 'blind, emaciated and consumptive', an austere religious ascetic like the Dalai Lama, and 'a crazy fellow who always carried four watches'.

The aristocratic demeanour and anachronistic politeness of Joyce as a man belied his popular reputation as a pornographer and writer of experimental masterpieces. His fellow writers and the smart expatriate set in Paris were taken aback by his primness and conventional moral attitudes. Whatever boundaries he might break in his art, in his private life Joyce was, or had resumed the status of, a devoted family man. Both he and Nora disliked the sexually liberated atmosphere of artistic and literary Paris during the 1920s. Although they accepted long-term lesbian and homosexual relationships, like that between Sylvia Beach and Adrienne Monnier, with equanimity, they had no patience with the adultery and casual promiscuity they often encountered amongst their acquaintances. The idolization of his literary admirers was flattering and useful, but Nora and the children were the bedrock of his life. As he would show in the coming years, Joyce could ruthlessly discard a friend whom he considered was threatening the interests of Nora, Giorgio or Lucia.

Thanks to the largesse of Harriet Weaver, the Irishman and his 'Celtic crew' – as Hemingway called the family – were living a life of unusual luxury. For almost a year they stayed in the opulent Victoria Palace hotel in Montparnasse, before moving into a large flat on the avenue Charles Floquet. Nora was now approaching forty, and had matured into a strong willed, sometimes shrewish, guardian of her self-indulgent husband. Many of Joyce's acquaintances underestimated her contribution, and thought that she should have taken more control of the family's domestic and financial affairs. Sylvia Beach believed that Harriet Weaver's gifts had added to the family's problems by allowing them a large income to squander. But it was unfair to expect Nora to develop any self-control about money, when so much of her life had been spent wondering where the next penny was coming from. Her apparent lack of interest in her husband's literary genius did not mean that she lacked appreciation of his financial success. But she was too aware of his human foibles to put him on any pedestal. Nora had a dry sense of humour, and enjoyed gently deflating Joyce in front of his circle of admiring acolytes; many of the more outrageous comments attributed to her were subtle leg-pulls in the best Irish tradition rather than sincerely meant. Nonetheless she was unenthusiastic about *Ulysses* and its successor, and considered them unreadable. She described *Finnegans Wake* as 'chop suey', and demanded to know: 'Why don't you write sensible books that people can understand?'

Joyce's children were approaching adulthood in the 1920s, and their future tribulations would place their father and mother under severe stress. Giorgio and Lucia had benefited from Joyce's new-found wealth, but their childhood had left them rootless and vulnerable. The family's poverty in Trieste, and their numerous moves from one country to the next, had left its mark on Joyce's son and daughter. By 1923 Giorgio had grown into a tall, good-looking youth, who spoke several languages fluently. After leaving school he had just taken up a career as a banker at the Banque National du Crédit, but was already tired of the job's monotony and long hours. His real interest lay in becoming an opera singer. Giorgio had inherited his father's vocal talents, and wanted to follow a career in music. With the encouragement and financial assistance of Joyce, who remembered his own miserable time at the Nast-Kolb and Schumacher bank in Rome, the young man gave in his notice and began studying at the Schola

Cantorum music academy. Lucia Joyce was still in school, but she was already causing her mother some concern. Joyce had often sung her to sleep in his arms during her infancy, and he still retained a very strong affection for his pretty, waif-like daughter. Yet she was insecure and prone to anxiety attacks, exacerbated by her many changes of home and school during the family's wanderings across Europe. Although the mental illness that was to blight her life was not yet apparent, Lucia's inability to communicate with her own age group, and her occasional eccentricities, hinted that all was not well with the girl.

After the publication of *Ulysses* Joyce was a notable celebrity on the Paris scene, but he avoided taking up the role of a literary lion. He refused to discuss both his own past works and those of his contemporaries, and steadfastly refused to speak at the receptions and lunches that were regularly held in his honour. This led to some embarrassing moments, as on the occasion he was introduced to the great French novelist Marcel Proust in 1922. It might have been expected that the two literary giants had much to talk about, but the meeting was a farce. Each obsessed by health matters, they discussed their respective stomach-aches, and each informed the other he was unfamiliar with his books. When Joyce became tipsy, the French novelist retreated to his bedroom, and the evening ended with a mutual friend persuading the boisterous Irishman to get a taxi home. But Joyce's simplicity and lack of pretension pleased others. When Le Corbusier was introduced to Joyce in 1937, for instance, the Irishman would talk only of two parakeets he had recently acquired. 'It is admirable that he talks about birds,' the great architect said afterwards.

Joyce did not forget his debt to two fellow writers who had influenced and helped him. He helped promote the neglected French writer Edouard Dujardin, who had first used the stream of consciousness technique in his novel *Les Lauriers Sont Coupés* ('The Laurels Have Been Cut Down') and brought some belated recognition to Italo Svevo – his old friend the Trieste factory owner Ettore Schmitz. In 1924 Schmitz wrote to Joyce in Paris, telling him that, at the age of sixty, he had just published a new novel, *Zeno*. He asked if Joyce could help him, since critics and the public alike had ignored the book. The Irish writer took up the cause of *Zeno,* and as a result the novel and its author received several enthusiastic reviews and articles. Before then the novels of Italo Svevo had been almost unknown outside Trieste, but by the time of his death in a car crash in 1928 his international reputation was well-established.

During his correspondence with Schmitz, Joyce mentioned that he had allotted a small role in his next book to his fellow writer's beautiful red-haired wife Livia. 'They say I have immortalized Svevo,' he told a journalist, 'but I've also immortalized the tresses of Signora Svevo. These were long and reddish brown … The river at Dublin passes dye-houses and so has reddish water. So I have playfully compared these two things in the book I'm writing. A lady in it will have the tresses which are really Signora Svevo's.' The 'lady' to whom he was referring was Anna Livia, wife of H. C. Earwicker and mother of the twins Shem and Shaun and their sister Isabel. In his scheme for *Finnegans Wake* this family were to be the characters at the centre of his 'universal history'. In the shifting, dream-like fabric of the book, they exist at a number of levels, manifesting in different guises in the flow of time and history. Joyce's conception of his new work took as its starting point the ancient Irish hero Finn MacCumhall lying dead beside the river Liffey (according to legend Finn is buried on the Hill of Howth, north of Dublin). The history of the world and Ireland flows dreamily through his fading consciousness. Finn MacCumhall is not merely a hero; he is also a god, a mountain, and the prototype of H. C. Earwicker and all men of action. Similarly Anna Livia is at different times a fertility goddess, the river Liffey, and all housewives and mothers. Shem and Shaun are all brothers and rivals from Cain and Abel onwards, whilst Isabel is the model of all seductive and desirable women. Around his archetypal family Joyce began weaving his punning tapestry of neologisms and historical references.

The writing of *Finnegans Wake* progressed quickly at first, partly because Joyce had a huge store of unused notes and research from *Ulysses*, which he was able to incorporate in the new work. By the beginning of 1924 he already had quite large segments of several chapters completed. Following the problems caused by the serialization of his earlier novel, it was not his original intention to publish any extracts from the book until it was completed. In October 1923, however, he received a visit from the American writer Ford Madox Ford, who was editing a new magazine, the *Transatlantic Review*. Ford strongly wished to include a piece by Joyce in his first issue, and pressed him to contribute something from the new book. After much hemming and hawing the Irish writer consented to give him a chapter, on the condition that he would be allowed to double proof it before publication. Not surprisingly, given Joyce's habit of making changes on his text before allowing it to be printed, there were so many difficulties preparing the extract that it was not ready for the magazine's inaugural issue in January 1924. But in April 1924 the first extract of Joyce's 'Work in Progress' was finally published, to the confusion of most of its readers. Further extracts would appear intermittently in reviews or as small volumes over the coming years. Many of these were in the periodical *transition*, edited by Joyce's Parisian friends Eugene and Maria Jolas. Between 1928 and 1937 they published seventeen instalments of the book.

The consternation caused by the first 'Work in Progress' extracts is understandable. To the uninitiated they seemed no more than a mish-mash of unconnected phrases, punctuated by meaningless words. What easy sense could a reader make of 'nor avoice from a afire bellowed mishe to tauftauf thuartpeatrick' or 'Rot a peck of pa's malt had Shem or Shen brewed by arclight and rory end to the regginbrow was to be seen ringsome on the waterface.' It appeared nonsensical, but in fact Joyce has chosen every word and phrase with tremendous care. *Finnegans Wake* was intended to be a comic novel by its author. It drew on his vast range of reading and on his tremendous knowledge of linguistics and history. Beneath its surface appearance of apparent gobbledygook was a profound depth of meaning and intention. Joyce's book, although almost painfully incomprehensible at times, was the disciplined creation of a master writer working carefully to his own interior plan and logic. If the Irishman used the sledgehammer of his genius to smash the English language to pieces, it was very much in the spirit of the iconoclastic cultural movements of the era. Joyce's vast experiment was the literary equivalent of the paintings of Salvadore Dali, Miro and Braque, the conceptual art of Marcel Duchamp, or the music of George Arnheim, one of whose compositions was scored for seven grand pianos, saws, hammers and an aeroplane propeller.

Regardless of the inner qualities of Joyce's great work, it was too much for Ezra Pound and Harriet Weaver to cope with. In November 1926 Pound wrote to Joyce after reading an extract. He told him that 'up to present I make nothing of it whatever … And in any case I don't see what which has to do with where …' Joyce's patroness felt much the same way about the extracts she was sent. The novelist carefully included a key that painstakingly explained the meanings of his allusions and new words, but she was not impressed. In 1927 she complained that: 'I do not care much for your Wholesale Safety Pun Factory nor for the darkness and unintelligibilities of your deliberately entangled language. It seems to me that you are wasting your genius.' Joyce was disconcerted, and began wondering whether he had gone astray in writing with such an incomprehensible style. He momentarily doubted his own sanity, and asked the critic Robert McAlmon if he considered him a madman. But after some reflection Joyce decided that 'the night world can't be represented in the language of day'. In his mind the new work was a natural progression from *Ulysses*, and to compromise its language and construction would destroy its value. Regardless of any criticism of its 'obscurity' (and there were to be many) he would follow the course he had chosen for his book.

There was an element of stubborn courage about Joyce's decision to continue working on the 'Work in Progress', especially as his eyes had been causing him much suffering. In 1924 and 1925 he had undergone a series of operations to try and save his fading sight. For long periods of those two years he was almost blind, and forced to use three magnifying glasses when writing or proofing his work. At the end of 1925 Dr Borsch performed his ninth operation to try and save the writer's vision, but it was not until well into the following year that Joyce had any respite from his eye trouble. In the midst of these problems he received news from Dublin that his aunt Josephine, the closest of his Dublin relatives after his father, was dying. To his great regret they had been estranged since 1922, when Nora had failed to visit the old woman on her way home after the aborted trip to Galway. In addition Mrs Murray had not forgiven her nephew for writing such a 'disgusting' book. On hearing of his aunt's illness Joyce wrote an exquisite letter of reconciliation, thanking her for her kindness to him after his mother's death, and stating that '... I am still attached to you by many bonds, of gratitude and affection and of respect as well ...'

Another less than sympathetic response to his current work came from his brother Stanislaus, who visited him in April 1926. In early 1925 Nora had found a new unfurnished flat at Square Robiac, near the Rue de Grenelle in the seventh arrondissement of Paris. For the first time since Trieste the couple wanted to set up a real home, rather than continue a wandering existence flitting between squalid flats and hotel rooms. They were comfortably off for the moment, and had acquired a circle of lively and amusing friends in the French capital. The six years that Joyce and Nora spent in this flat was the longest period they stayed in any of their Paris homes, and encompassed one of the more stable times of their life together. But Stanislaus, when he came to Paris, carried too many grudges to be impressed with his brother's new prosperity and fame. In his eyes James was rich and pampered, and he frowned upon his brother's continued heavy drinking and extravagant use of Harriet Weaver's money. Stanislaus found his brother's friends sycophantic, and thought they were too eager to praise his literary work. He was not afraid to tell Joyce he disliked *Ulysses*, finding it over-elaborate and crudely vulgar in parts. *Finnegans Wake* was totally incomprehensible to him: 'You have done the longest day in literature, and now you are conjuring up the deepest night', Stanislaus told his brother with some venom. It was, one can guess, with great relief that Joyce saw Stanislaus back off to Trieste. The soul-mate of James's younger years had become a carping antagonist – truly Shaun the postman to his Shem the penman.

Joyce may have regretted the breach with Stanislaus, but it became another strand to weave into the extraordinary fabric of *Finnegans Wake*. Nevertheless they were still brothers, and the ties that bound them could never be fully severed. Six months after Stanislaus returned to Trieste, he wrote to announce that he was going to be married to a girl named Nelly Lichtensteiger within the next year. Joyce had hardly digested this information when he received an urgent request from his sister Eileen, who was on holiday in Dublin. She was stranded there, and needed a loan so she could get back to her home in Trieste. The reason for the predicament, Joyce learnt from Stanislaus, was that whilst she was away her husband Frantisek Schaurek had committed suicide, following the failure of his business. When Eileen, unaware that she was a widow, visited him in Paris on her way to Italy, Joyce could not bring himself to tell her about the tragedy. She arrived in Trieste expecting to meet her husband, and at first refused to believe he was dead. It was only when the body was exhumed and shown to her that Eileen accepted the truth, afterwards suffering a breakdown that left her confined to hospital for months.

After the criticism of 'Work in Progress' from Stanislaus, Ezra Pound and Harriet Weaver, Joyce felt he should appease his readers with a more accessible example of his talents. He had continued to write poetry over the years, and had assembled thirteen that he considered worth publishing. They showed a different side of James Joyce's mastery of language to _Ulysses_ or the labyrinthine new novel. Sylvia Beach agreed to print the slim volume, which appeared in 1927. Joyce titled it _Pomes Penyeach,_ since it cost a shilling and contained a baker's dozen of poems, but the publication received little critical or public attention. Ezra Pound's reaction to his verse collection reflected the widening gulf between the American and Joyce. Never one to temper his views, Pound wrote back that he thought they were not worth publishing.

Whatever disappointments he may have experienced with reactions to 'Work in Progress', Joyce's international reputation was now assured. The French edition of _A Portrait of the Artist as a Young Man_ (translated by Jenny Serruys) appeared in 1924 under the title _Dédalus,_ and from 1923 onwards several French writers (principally Auguste Morel) began the almost superhuman task of rendering _Ulysses_ into the language of Joyce's adopted country. This French translation took many years to finish to its author's satisfaction, and only finally reached the public in 1929. To mark its appearance Adrienne Monnier arranged a luncheon in the countryside outside of Versailles, which she called the 'Déjeuner _Ulysse_'. The guests included the French writers Edouard Dujardin and Paul Valéry, along with a disciple of Joyce's, at that time still unknown, Samuel Beckett. The young Irishman was already a regular visitor to the Joyce's flat on his frequent trips from Dublin to Paris, and his growing intimacy with the family would soon have unfortunate results.

Whilst the publication of *Ulysses* in French translation was a landmark in the book's history, the situation in the United States went from bad to worse. Following the successful obscenity case against the *Little Review* in 1919, the novel had achieved legendary status in that country. For years most of Shakespeare and Company's sales of the novel in Paris were to curious American visitors seeking a copy of the unobtainable masterpiece to bring home. Then, in 1926, an American acquaintance of Ezra Pound named Phillip Roth used a loophole in the copyright laws to pirate most of the banned novel. Roth, without receiving Joyce's permission or paying him, began serializing a slightly expurgated version of the novel in his magazine *Two Worlds Monthly*. Joyce, with the support of almost every other writer in Europe and America, objected vehemently to this blatant commercial robbery. He arranged for a petition, the 'International Protest', to be forwarded to leading figures in literature, science and the arts. It was signed by 167 of them, including Albert Einstein, H. G. Wells, Sean O'Casey, W. B. Yeats, Ernest Hemingway, D. H. Lawrence. The 'International Protest' was issued on 2 February 1927 (Joyce's birthday), but Roth ignored the petition and continued publishing instalments from his exorcised *Ulysses*. It was not until November 1927 that Joyce's lawyers were able to obtain a temporary injunction ordering him to stop. A year later a court decision barred Roth from using Joyce's name or literary works in the future, but because of a legal technicality the author was unable to seek any recompense for the previous infringements of his copyright. The debacle once more reminded the frustrated author of the huge potential market for *Ulysses* in the United States, if the authorities would lift the ban.

As the 1920s progressed, and he became world-famous, Joyce became surrounded by admirers who helped and ran errands for him. Whilst he may have distanced himself from Ireland, Joyce remained obsessed by his country, and counted several Irishmen amongst his closest friends. James Stephens, the tiny writer of *The Crock of Gold,* shared his fellow Dubliner's wry humour and flamboyant imagination. During his creative crisis over the direction of *Finnegans Wake,* Joyce seriously considered asking Stephens to take over finishing the book for him. His connection with Padraic Colum also became more important. Their first meetings in the early 1900s had been fraught with tension, mainly because of Joyce's consuming urge at that period to demolish the work of the Irish Literary Revival. But during the 1920s, when Colum moved to Paris with his wife Mary, they struck up a warm friendship. The Colums provided loyal support to the writer and Nora through a succession of domestic crises in the later part of his life, and he remained grateful for the help and sympathy they gave him.

The first of these crises concerned Nora, who had enjoyed perfect health until 1928. In that year she was suddenly diagnosed as suffering from cancer, and underwent an exploratory operation and radium treatment, which left her health problems unresolved. In February 1929 she again returned to hospital, where her surgeons performed a hysterectomy. Joyce, who had an intense fear of cancer after watching his mother die, insisted on having a bed placed beside his wife's in the hospital. Fortunately the operation was a success, and Nora recovered without any complications, but the illness confirmed how much Joyce depended upon his spouse in all aspects of his life. Nora, even if she sometimes talked to him with contempt, was the only person with whom he could drop all his emotional defences and admit his fears for the future. She alone brought a degree of stability into his chaotic personal life, and nagged him to keep his self-destructive drinking under some control. Her great value to him was that her concern was James Joyce the man rather than James Joyce the writer. Without that rock mooring him to reality, the troubled writer was a rudderless ship adrift in a storm-tossed sea.

In February 1930 Joyce heard of a brilliant Swiss eye-surgeon in Zurich named Alfred Vogt, who was reputed to achieve brilliant results with his daring techniques. In May of that year Vogt removed a cataract on Joyce's left eye, and from then onwards he performed a series of operations on the writer. Joyce continued to visit Vogt for treatment throughout the 1930s. The Swiss surgeon probably saved his patient from going entirely blind, although Joyce's eyes continued to cause him considerable pain and discomfort at times. Alfred Vogt never charged the writer for his services, and was instrumental in getting Joyce permission to enter Switzerland when he had difficulty obtaining a resident's permit in 1940.

Joyce and Nora were now well into middle age, and as the children approached adulthood, their close-knit family life began to disintegrate. Giorgio left the family nest first, and caused his parents some concern when they discovered he was involved with a woman Nora thought unsuitable for him. Helen Kastor Fleischman was typical of many American émigrées in Paris at the time. Her New York family, the Kastors, was of German Jewish descent, but like many wealthy Americans of her generation she was attracted to the intellectual and artistic excitement of post-war Paris. The sophisticated New Yorker was drawn like a magnet to the literary 'stars' of the Modernist movement, and soon joined the group of admirers around Joyce. She and Nora became quite close, and Helen encouraged Nora to modernize her wardrobe, since Nora's tastes were old-fashioned by contemporary standards. She brought Nora to the studios of the most exclusive dress designers, and helped her choose new outfits. Nora was unaware at first that her friend had seduced her twenty-one year old son, and then led him into a passionate love affair. The young man's mother was less than happy for several reasons when she found out. Helen was still officially married, even if she and her husband were more or less estranged; she also had a child. Moreover she was in her early thirties when the affair began, and not everybody trusted her motives in pursuing the son of James Joyce. Her sister-in-law, for instance, described Helen as a 'sexual vampire', and implied that Giorgio's main attraction in her eyes was his famous father. This was unfair since Helen's later psychological problems suggest she was genuine in her feelings towards Giorgio, but Nora felt that the strong-willed and over-excitable American was an unsuitable partner for her emotionally inexperienced son.

Helen and Giorgio nevertheless married, but not until 1930, since it was necessary for her to get a divorce from her first husband. Joyce was less worried than Nora about his son's choice of a bride. He liked his new daughter-in-law's vibrant humour, and hoped that her family could use their influence in New York to help him find a publisher for *Ulysses*. Nora was not convinced the marriage would last, but could console herself that Helen was rich, and came from an impeccable social background. She was more worried about her daughter Lucia, who was already displaying the signs of a serious psychological disorder, although neither of her parents would accept it. Joyce had spoilt both his children materially, but failed to prepare them for the reality of living under the shadow of a famous father. He had encouraged Lucia to follow her chosen career of becoming a dancer after leaving school, and she did well in her studies for three years. But in 1929 Lucia made an emotional declaration that she lacked the ability to be a professional ballerina, and stopped dancing altogether. Joyce did not question her sudden change in mood, even though she was obviously in great distress, and simply took it for granted that his daughter would quickly find another outlet for her creative talents.

Because his distorted vision matched Lucia's in many ways, Joyce could not comprehend that a malaise more serious than the confusion of youth was behind her irrational statements and lack of focus. But outsiders noticed the dark tides that were rising in Lucia's psyche. A lady doctor observed the Joyce family eating at a Paris restaurant one night. 'If I was the mother of James Joyce's daughter,' she commented, 'and saw her staring off into space in that way, I'd be very concerned about it.' In the decade to come Joyce was acknowledged as one of the century's greatest literary geniuses. Yet no adulation could balance out the personal sorrows he would endure, the saddest of which was the tragic illness of his daughter Lucia. Hemmed in on all sides by his troubles, he would stumble on obstinately towards his goal of completing

Finnegans Wake. James Joyce was not always a kind-hearted or noble man; often indeed he was selfish, petty and greedy. Nonetheless Joyce's last, abstruse book would be a testament to his refusal to bow either to the despair of madness, or the inevitability of death.

CHAPTER IX

A TROUBLED MAN

In May 1929 Shakespeare and Company published a strange little work entitled 'Our Exagmination round his Factification for Incamination of Work in Progress'. The volume consisted of twelve essays written by Joyce's admirers – amongst them Frank Budgen, Eugene Jolas and Samuel Beckett – defending *Finnegans Wake* against the attacks of its chief critics. It was some indication of the prominence Joyce had achieved that these included the likes of Rebecca West, Sean O'Faolain and Wyndham Lewis. The book was Joyce's idea, and he had suggested most of the approaches followed in the various essays. The extracts of 'Work in Progress' that had already been published were attracting much interest in literary circles, and Joyce was eager to state the case for his experimentations with literary form and the English language. Shortly afterwards he arranged for the 'Black Sun' Press, a small Parisian publisher owned by the American expatriates Harry and Caresse Crosby, to publish his mock fable 'The Ondt and the Gracehoper', along with two other long pieces from the book, under the title 'Tales Told of Shem and Shaun'.

Joyce had become an international figure, and his slim form and ascetic face – invariably wearing spectacles and often with an eye patch over the damaged left eye – were known far beyond the artistic circles of Paris. Thomas Wolfe, who observed the family on a trip to the battlefield of Waterloo in 1926, described the famous Irishman in a letter to a friend.

'He was wearing a blind over one eye. He was very simply – even shabbily – dressed … Joyce got a bit stagey on the way home, draping his overcoat poetically around his shoulders. But I liked Joyce's looks, not extraordinary at first sight but growing. His face was highly coloured, slightly concave – his mouth thin, not delicate but extraordinarily humorous. He had a large powerful straight nose – redder than his face, somewhat pitted with scars and boils.'

Joyce's literary affairs were now far more complex than in the years of his obscurity, and he was not able to cope with them alone, especially with his deteriorating eyesight. Everybody who knew him was drawn into doing errands and procuring items or little luxuries he needed. From 1930 onwards his mainstay in dealing with his business correspondence was an expatriate Russian Jew named Paul Leon who had arrived in Paris after the First World War. Leon, a qualified lawyer, proved invaluable as an unpaid secretary, and dealt with Joyce's publishers' contracts and commercial dealings for most of the remainder of his life. Joyce was pleased to place his trust in his witty and likeable lawyer friend, whose Russian patronymic middle name – Leopoldovich – reminded him of Leopold Bloom. Leon was a friend of Helen Fleischman, and after her marriage to Giorgio became part of the family's social life. His devotion to Joyce's interests made him an invaluable asset in the writer's dealings with the world beyond his small circle of intimates.

146

The fact that Joyce and Nora were not legally married had long been buried from the public view. It was their secret, concealed by the lie that they had contracted a civil marriage shortly after leaving Ireland. Even their children were unaware of the truth until the late 1920s, when they were devastated to learn that they were illegitimate. The marriage of Giorgio to Helen Fleischman finally persuaded Joyce that he must sort out his and Nora's irregular situation. No matter how much he disliked the institution of marriage, it was necessary if he wished to avoid legal tangles over inheritance. There was also the danger of offending his son's wealthy American in-laws the Kastors, who might prove useful allies in the battle to get the ban on *Ulysses* lifted. In March 1931 Joyce's fears of public exposure were realized when the *Catholic World*, an American magazine, published an account of his elopement, and told its readers that Joyce did not 'grant Nora the protection of even a civil marriage'. With remarkable accuracy the article added that 'French testamentary law makes the position of the mistress and of the spurious offspring one of very great insecurity'. The writer of the piece was an Irishman named Michael Lennon, who appears to have acquired his information during a late-night drinking session with Joyce in Paris some months earlier.

By this time, however, Joyce was finally on the verge of marrying Nora. Some months previously he had written to Harriet Weaver explaining the situation and asking her to look into the inheritance laws in England. His patroness, after her initial surprise that Joyce had concealed the truth about his marital status for so long, consulted her solicitors and confirmed there was no legal impediment to the marriage being performed in England. This suited Joyce, who was worried about the rising cost of living in Paris, and had been considering leaving France for some months. In April 1931 Nora, James and Lucia left the flat in the seventh arrondissement where they had been living since 1925, and quietly slipped over to England. Harriet Weaver was waiting for them when they arrived. She had rented a small flat for them in Kensington. Whatever qualms she might have felt about _Finnegans Wake_ were put aside in the cause of helping Joyce and Nora legalize their union. Joyce's unique bond with Miss Weaver was strengthened by her willingness to help, and restored his confidence in her continued support for the future.

Joyce selected 1 July, the date of his father's birthday, for his wedding. With his usual cunning he decided to marry by licence, so that he would only have to give a day's notice before the ceremony, and thus avoid attracting any publicity. To his embarrassment the English press got hold of the story. Joyce woke up on the morning of 1 July to find news of his imminent marriage trumpeted in the morning papers under the headline 'Author to Wed'. His solicitor's explanation that: 'For testamentary reasons it was thought well that the partners should be married according to English law', sounded logical enough, but probably fooled none of the hard-bitten reporters who gathered outside Kensington Registry Office to interview and photograph the couple. Joyce's determination to conceal the illegitimacy of his children nearly stopped the wedding going ahead. He insisted to the registrar that he and Nora had been married in 1904. Then how, the registrar replied, could he expect to marry Nora if they were already legally husband and wife? The day was saved when the couple's solicitor hastily intervened, and explained that the earlier marriage was not recognized in English law. To everybody's relief the ceremony was allowed to go ahead.

Joyce was mortified by the attention he had drawn on himself, especially when his wedding photograph appeared in the papers and a crowd of reporters camped outside of his small flat. 'I certainly do not want a score of journalists with pencils in their hands intruding where they are not wanted …' he wrote anxiously to Harriet Weaver when telling her of his plans for a secret wedding. He now found himself under siege from the Press, and the object of gossip in Paris, Dublin and Galway as well as London. Nora, on the other hand, was more amused than upset by the debacle. After their long years together, and the rearing of two children, the belated wedding seemed almost farcical. It had been years, indeed, since she had had a sexual relationship with her new 'husband'. 'I felt a proper fool', she laughingly replied when asked about her reaction to finding reporters waiting at the Registrar's office.

Joyce was feted and treated with great respect by the London literary establishment, but soon tired of the British capital. In September he returned to Paris with his wife and daughter. He was in consultation with a number of publishers, both for *Finnegans Wake'*(when it was finished) and the still banned *Ulysses*. He was happy to sign contracts with his long-time associate B. W. Huebsch (now with the Viking Press) for the former, but procuring an American edition of *Ulysses* posed a number of unresolved legal issues. The cost of challenging the legal ban on selling the book might be prohibitive, and there was no guarantee that it would succeed. Sylvia Beach would also have to receive something, since she had been publishing her Shakespeare and Company edition of the book for nearly a decade, and held the rights on it. Joyce, still toiling away on *Finnegans Wake,* left the delicate negotiations with American publishers to his son's New York brother-in-law Robert Kastor.

In December 1931 news arrived that John Joyce lay dying in a Dublin hospital. James Joyce even now refused to return to Ireland, but kept in daily communication to check on his father's condition. The old man breathed his last on 27 December, reviving on his deathbed to ask his relatives to 'Tell Jim that he was born at 6.30 in the morning'. The message was a belated reply to an earlier request from his eldest son, who was having his horoscope drawn up by an astrologer, and needed his exact time of birth. Joyce's last strong link with Dublin was severed. The death removed the single greatest influence on his childhood. In many ways James Joyce replicated his father's vices of drunkenness and unthinking selfishness, but he had risen above them to fulfil the creative promise that John Joyce had squandered by his indolence. 'I got from him his portraits, a waistcoat, a good tenor voice and a licentious disposition (out of which however the greater part of any talent I may have springs), but apart from these something I cannot define', he wrote. Joyce, alone amongst his brothers and sisters, had continued to love and understand his father into adulthood. John Joyce always looked upon his eldest son as his favourite child, despite his desertion to the Continent. He followed James's rise to fame with pride, even if he was aware that it was unlikely they would ever meet again. In his will the old man ignored his daughters and Stanislaus, and left all of his estate of £500 to his wayward writer son.

Joyce was saddened by the knowledge that his father had

never praised any of his books. An even greater sorrow was that they had not seen each other for so many years. In letters to his friends he blamed his omission to visit his father on his fear of returning to Dublin. 'He loved me deeply, more and more as he grew older' Joyce wrote to Ezra Pound 'but in spite of my own feelings I never dared to trust myself into the hands of my enemies.' He expressed similar feelings when writing to T. S. Eliot; '... quite lately I have had experience of malignancy and treachery on the part of people to whom I have done nothing but friendly acts' he stated, referring to Lennon's abuse of his confidences in the *Catholic World* article, 'I did not feel myself safe and my wife and son opposed me going to Dublin.' Later in 1932 he took the opportunity to snub his homeland when W. B. Yeats invited him to join the newly founded 'Irish Academy of Letters' along with W. B. Shaw. It was a great compliment to be considered the equal of Shaw and Yeats, both by now Nobel Prize winners, but Joyce wished to have nothing to do with Ireland, although he thanked Yeats for past kindnesses. 'My case, however, being as it was and probably will be I see no reason at all why my name should have arisen in connection with such an academy,' he replied.

So all-consuming was Joyce's grief for his father that he again considered abandoning *Finnegans Wake*. 'Why go on writing about a place I did not dare to go at such a moment?' he wrote to Harriet Weaver after his failure to attend his father's deathbed. His real problem was guilt, as he admitted in the same letter: 'I knew he was old. But I thought he would live longer. It is not his death that crushed me so much but self-accusation.' Several months passed before the depression was lifted by a joyful event that balanced out his great sense of loss. On February 15 1932 Helen gave birth to a son, Joyce's grandchild, who was named Stephen James Joyce in his honour. To the grieving Irishman it was a sign of forgiveness for his dereliction of duty to his father. Shortly afterwards he sat down and wrote 'Ecce Puer' – the exquisite short poem in which he celebrated the arrival of the new life and mourned the passing of the old. Its last verse expressed his mingled joy and grief with great simplicity and beauty.

> 'A child is sleeping
> An old man gone
> O father forsaken
> Forgive your son.'

Shortly after the birth Giorgio and Helen asserted their independence by secretly slipping off to church and baptizing their infant son against Joyce's express wishes. Giorgio, or George as he was now generally known, was suffering from being constantly in the shadow of his renowned father. Joyce had not always been an easy parent, and he was sometimes hard on Giorgio, whose rather serious character bore more in common with Stanislaus than his own father. Possibly the young man had been hurt by Joyce's almost obsessive promotion of John Sullivan, an Irish opera singer whom he had first heard in Paris in 1930. Sullivan was a fine performer, but Joyce's enthusiasm was rooted in his identification with a fellow Irishman fighting to make his way against prejudice and indifference. But in pushing forward Sullivan he seemed to neglect the career of his own son, another professional singer who was struggling for recognition. There may have been a small element of jealousy in this, since Joyce was still proud of his own singing, and regretful that he had not made more of it. Giorgio made little progress singing in France, and in 1934, with the encouragement of Helen, he decided to move to the United States and try his luck there. Although he returned to Paris after a couple of years, and was with his father during his last months, his departure left another gap in Joyce's small family circle.

The birth of Joyce's grandson was preceded by another domestic upheaval. On the afternoon of 2 February 1932 (Joyce's birthday) Lucia turned on Nora and threw a chair at her. It was the most serious sign yet of her growing mental derangement. After leaving her dancing career Lucia had drifted into a directionless and self-destructive existence. She was now in her mid-twenties, but was becoming increasingly alienated from the world around her. Joyce encouraged his fragile daughter's work as an illustrator; in 1931 she was commissioned at his bequest to design lettrines for a volume called 'The Joyce Book' that was going to be published in England. But in her personal life the emotionally vulnerable young woman had become promiscuous and prone to erratic behaviour. Joyce still refused to admit that she was in need of help, and pretended to himself that all was well with the young woman. Nora, on the other hand, could not avoid seeing that Lucia was running wild. But her occasional tongue-lashings served only to provoke the girl's increasingly open hatred of her mother.

At least part of Lucia's spiralling decline may be laid at the door of her unrequited passion for Samuel Beckett, who was a regular visitor to their flat. Beckett was a stunningly attractive man to women, but by his own account he had no experience of the opposite sex at this time of his life. Over a

period of several years he saw much of Joyce's daughter, and
occasionally took her out to the cinema and lunch. But he
was not sexually interested in Lucia, and was embarrassed
when he learnt of her passion for him. He brusquely rejected
the girl's romantic advances, and told her that the only reason
he came to the house was to spend time with her father.
Nora, on seeing Lucia's hopes harshly shattered by the young
Irishman, was furious, and accused him of leading her gulli-
ble daughter on. She complained to her husband about
Beckett's behaviour, and insisted he be barred from their home.
Beckett was only allowed back into the family's circle a year
later, after Lucia's first major breakdown revealed her basic
instability. It should be mentioned that the future Nobel Prize
winner treated Joyce's tragic daughter with great kindness
after she was hospitalized, and kept an eye on her well-being
until her death in 1982.

After Lucia's attack on Nora, the problem of her mental
condition had to be confronted. Giorgio insisted that he take
his sister to a clinic, and after a few days rest she seemed to
have recovered. Nora believed that marriage would solve
Lucia's psychological difficulties, and Paul Leon cast his net
around for a suitable candidate. The choice fell on his brother-
in-law Alex Ponisovsky, who was inveigled into proposing.
Lucia accepted, but her parents' casual manipulation of her
emotions ended catastrophically. On the day of her engage-
ment party in April 1932, the young woman fell into a cata-
tonic state from which she could not be revived at first. Lucia
was removed to a mental hospital to be treated for a schizo-
phrenic disorder. Once again Joyce was consumed with guilt,
blaming himself both for passing on the seeds of the illness,
and for not providing a stable and settled environment for his

children to grow up in. He threw himself into trying to find help for his daughter, and in the coming years would trail her around consultants and clinics across Europe looking for a cure for her incurable illness. Yet another obstacle had arisen to impede the progress of 'Work in Progress'.

In the midst of this domestic turmoil Robert Kastor arrived from New York, having struck a deal with an American publisher who was eager to challenge the legal ban on *Ulysses*. In March 1931 Joyce agreed terms with Bennett Cerf of Random House, and received a substantial advance on the future American edition of the novel. Sadly, the deal gave a fatal blow to his friendship with Sylvia Beach. Shakespeare and Company had been giving him a steady if not spectacular income from *Ulysses* for years. Still it was ridiculous that the most important novel in English of the time could only be acquired from a small bookshop in Paris. That situation could not continue, yet the matter of compensating Sylvia Beach if she surrendered her publisher's rights needed to be resolved. The bookshop owner had, after all, made a large investment in Joyce, both emotional and financial. For almost a decade she had endured his unremitting harassment for advance payments, whilst supporting him through a succession of personal and professional crises. Her pent-up annoyance at the ungrateful author's endless importuning was reflected in an angry letter written to him by her partner Adrienne Monnier in May 1931, in response to yet another request for royalties. The letter's main accusation, which stung Joyce to the core, was that he pretended to have no interest in fame and wealth, while secretly being obsessed with them. 'What Gide doesn't know' she wrote, referring to a comment by the French author that Joyce was almost saintly in his determination not to compromise his work, '… is that you are, on the contrary very concerned with success and money … In Paris rumour has it that you are spoiled, that we have ruined you with overwhelming praise.'

By the early 1930s Sylvia Beach was quite happy to break her professional connection with Joyce, especially as her business had been doing badly and she wanted to retire. In fact, whilst Joyce and Nora were living in luxury, she had been struggling to survive. But she believed Shakespeare and Company deserved some recompense for its devotion to his interests. When the possibility of an American edition of *Ulysses* was first mentioned in 1930, Miss Beach demanded $25,000 for the world rights. No publisher was willing to pay this huge sum, and she was pressurized to release the book for nothing. When Padraic Colum told her 'Ya're standing in Joyce's way', she eventually gave up her interest in the novel, although she was allowed to retain a small percentage of the royalties of the European edition. Considering the large sums Joyce was to receive from the American edition, he had treated Sylvia Beach shabbily. His ruthlessness left her feeling cheated, and although the rift between them was never openly expressed, their close association was permanently broken.

With Sylvia Beach off the scene, Joyce's American publisher could begin the legal challenge to lift the ban on *Ulysses*. There was no guarantee that the case would succeed, but two factors were in its favour. The first lay in American society, which had changed considerably in its attitudes, and was far more tolerant than in 1919. The second was Joyce's own reputation; he was now a revered master of modern literature, rather than a controversial and unknown newcomer. The second trial of the novel on obscenity charges was heard in the New York District Court in the autumn of 1933. Joyce's lawyers argued cogently that the novel was a modern classic, citing leading critics and authors like Rebecca West, Arnold Bennett and Edmund Wilson in their support. Judge John M. Woolsey, who understood the importance of the case, had spent six months reading the disputed novel. On 6 December he ruled that *Ulysses* could be admitted into the United States. 'I am quite aware,' he concluded 'that owing to some of its scenes *Ulysses* is a rather strong draught to ask some sensitive, though normal, persons to take. But my considered opinion, after long reflection, is that whilst in many places the effect of *Ulysses* on the reader undoubtedly is somewhat emetic, nowhere does it tend to be aphrodisiac.' The lifting of the ban, confirmed by the US Supreme Court after an appeal, was an important landmark in the history of literature in the twentieth century, and a huge personal victory for Joyce. Since the early 1900s he had often been muzzled by publishers, printers and official censors who disapproved of what he wrote – from early articles at UCD, through *Dubliners,* and *Portrait,* and at last to *Ulysses*. Often Joyce had dreamed that he would one day be publicly vindicated, and his oppressors proved to be in the wrong. The Woolsey decision gave him this long hoped-for moment, and justified his refusal to expurgate his books in the name of avoiding prosecution. In 1934 the first American edition of *Ulysses* was published by Random House.

Joyce's great novel was now becoming readily available in most civilized countries. In Europe the freeing of the copyright led to a new edition, published under the imprint of the Odyssey Press of Hamburg. Sylvia Beach was allowed to retain a percentage of these royalties, and in addition Joyce presented her with the manuscript of *Stephen Hero*, the early novel that later was transformed into *Portrait*. He dismissed the book as 'rubbish', but on its posthumous publication *Stephen Hero* was recognized as a worthy addition to the Joycean canon. The Odyssey Press employed Stuart Gilbert, an associate of Joyce who had translated his works into French, to edit and correct the flawed Shakespeare and Company edition of *Ulysses*. He removed many mistakes from the original published text, with the result that the Odyssey Press edition is considered the most accurate early version of the novel. The ban on publishing the book in England remained, but in late 1933 Joyce was informed that the Prime Minister and the Attorney General were not planning to mount a legal challenge to its publication there. After some delays an English edition, published by John Lane, went on open sale in 1936. There was also a huge demand to read the novel from non-English speakers across the world. By the time of Joyce's death in 1940 his greatest work was available in French, Danish, Italian, German and Japanese translations.

By the 1930s academic and critical assessments of Joyce's novel were beginning to appear – the precursors of a vast range of scholarly works on every aspect of his writings. Stuart Gilbert published the first major critical analysis of *Ulysses*, in 1930. In 1934 a second important study appeared when Frank Budgen – Joyce's confidant in the period when he was writing the novel – published *James Joyce and the Making of Ulysses*. The earliest full-length biographical study of Joyce was Herbert Gorman's *James Joyce; the First Forty Years*, published in the United States by B. W. Huebsch in 1924. Some years later Joyce asked Gorman to write an authorized biography of his life, based mainly on information given by himself.

Gorman began interviewing his subject in 1930, but almost a decade passed before the book was finished. Joyce's 'official' version of his life was less than honest in places; it glossed over his father's extravagance, for instance, and maintained that a marriage with Nora had taken place in 1904, just after their elopement. The book was also vindictive towards many of his former friends. Joyce's tales of their 'betrayals' left the impression that almost everybody he had ever trusted had turned against him. There was something unpleasant about the way he paid off old scores in Gorman's book, but a more sympathetic picture of his faults and virtues could be found in his letters to Harriet Weaver. There Joyce portrayed himself in the round, unashamedly revealing his greed and pettiness alongside his humour, artistic honesty and insight into the human condition.

Lucia's problems in the mid-1930s were a major hindrance to the progress of *Finnegans Wake*, which seemed to drag on interminably. In June 1934 Joyce completed and corrected 'The Mime of Mick Nick and the Maggies', Chapter IX of his long book, for publication by the Servire Press. Joyce never abandoned working on the new book, but he was plagued by worry and near-blindness. He was assisted by Mme France Raphael, whose task it was to rewrite his almost illegible scrawl in very large letters so that he could correct the text. His visual impairment slowed Joyce's work-rate to a crawl, yet in fits and starts his manuscript was inexorably heading towards its magnificent concluding passages, where the Liffey flows into the Irish Sea, and life is changed into death. Joyce was almost transcending language in his search to express his nighttime landscape in sound and rhythm. 'Heaven knows what my prose means,' he wrote to Lucia, 'but it's pleasing to the ear … and that's enough for me.' Whatever doubts he may once have harboured about the direction of the novel were long behind him. 'I can justify every line of my book'; and 'I can do anything with language' – comments made to Samuel Beckett – reflected his satisfaction with his progress. Yet the agonizing search for a cure for Lucia, with its trail of false hopes and crushing disappointments, drained his diminishing energies.

Joyce removed his daughter from hospital a week after her breakdown and brought her back to Paris, where she continued her treatment at home. He tried to keep a semblance of normality, encouraging Lucia to continue drawing her ornate letters; some had already appeared in a special edition of *Pomes Penyeach* (1932) and he would later pay to print a second book of her lettrines, *A Chaucer A.B.C.* (1936). Lucia remained extremely volatile, however, and was prone to hysterical fits and violent outbursts; on several occasions she ran away and had to be returned by the police. The situation could not go on indefinitely, and became intolerable on the day of Joyce's fifty-second birthday in February 1934. Lucia, upset that Joyce was expecting an important call, cut the phone line to their flat, then impulsively slapped her mother's face. Nora refused to have her uncontrollable daughter near her any more, and she was sent to a sanatorium at Prangins, near Geneva, for a long stay. Whilst she was settling in her parents took the opportunity to take a long driving holiday with some friends, but on their return they found there was no improvement in her mental condition. Joyce transferred Lucia to a hospital near Zurich for treatment; after a few weeks the doctors there admitted they could not help, and suggested he take her elsewhere. Joyce refused to accept Lucia's sickness was incurable, and brought her to the clinic of the renowned Swiss psycho-analyst Carl Gustav Jung at Kussnacht.

Joyce had known of Jung since the years he spent in Zurich during World War I. His financial sponsor Edith McCormick had tried to persuade him to go to Jung for analysis, and Joyce believed the Swiss psychologist was behind her decision to cut off his monthly allowance after he refused. In those days Joyce professed to dislike the theories of Jung and Freud ('the Swiss Tweedledum and the Austrian Tweedledee' as he once described them), which he had read and discounted in Trieste. But in 1932 Jung sent Joyce a letter in which he stated his admiration for *Ulysses* and praised Molly Bloom's stream of consciousness monologue. '… The forty pages of non stop run in the end is a string of veritable psychological peaches. I suppose the devil's grandmother knows as much about women. I didn't.' Joyce proudly showed the letter around his Paris friends, but Nora was sceptical. 'He knows nothing about women', she said of her husband. Jung hoped that he might find a key to unlock Lucia's insanity, but she would not allow the renowned psychoanalyst to hold a meaningful dialogue with her. After a promising but false start, he told Joyce that there was no point in accepting her as a patient. Jung afterwards made an interesting comparison between Joyce and his daughter. To others the Irishman had often seemed on the edge of madness, both in his literature and his life. But in Jung's opinion Joyce was not insane. He described the father and daughter as two people going to the bottom of a river; the difference was that one was diving and the other falling.

In 1935 Lucia went with Eileen Joyce Schaurek to stay in London with Harriet Weaver, in the belief that a change of environment might lead to an improvement. However she was soon causing havoc with her behaviour, and drove Miss Weaver to distraction. The situation got worse when Eileen deserted her niece and returned to Dublin. Joyce was hostile and dismissive when his patroness reported that his daughter had run away on several occasions, and was now demanding plastic surgery on her chin. In his opinion these were minor matters that hardly compared to Lucia's bouts of madness in Paris, or her attacks on her mother. He was convinced his efforts had healed Lucia's mental illness, and would not countenance the seriousness of her current mental aberrations. Joyce suggested that Lucia should be sent to Ireland, where she could stay with Eileen at her house in Bray, the seaside resort he remembered from his early childhood. The change did not help, and Lucia's antics included dangerous pranks like lighting a turf fire on her aunt's living-room carpet. Then she absconded from Eileen's care, and was missing for six days before Joyce's sisters Eva and Florence retrieved her from a Dublin police station. Lucia was placed in an asylum at her own request, and Joyce asked Maria Jolas, a close family friend, to travel to Dublin and assess her condition. Under her care Lucia was brought back to England, where Miss Weaver had rented a cottage in the country, and was waiting with a nurse to look after her.

It was unreasonable of Joyce to expect the restrained middle-aged woman to tend for his irrational twenty-eight-year-old daughter, who was so spoiled she needed to be pampered like a small child. By December 1935 Lucia was a danger to herself and others, and Joyce's friends persuaded him to let Miss Weaver send her to a mental hospital in Northampton for 'tests'. What followed was at once farcical and very sad.

Harriet Weaver, conscientious as ever, examined the patient's chart. She mistakenly thought that it indicated Lucia was suffering from cancer, and informed her father. His manic fear of the disease led Joyce to turn sarcastically on his patroness when he found out she had made an error. The incident was a further milestone in the decline of their long collaboration, which was now grinding to an uncomfortable halt. To an extent they had outgrown one another and the breach was inevitable. Miss Weaver was a committed member of the Communist Party, and most of her wealth was being directed towards financing its aims and projects. She felt that she had met her obligations to the prickly Irish writer. His work, in addition, had lost something of its appeal to her. Try as she might, she found 'Work in Progress' tedious, and thought it was an unworthy sequel to *Ulysses*. It was not in Miss Weaver's nature to entirely desert her adopted writer, but she let their correspondence dwindle away to nothing with few regrets.

Joyce was still unwilling to see Lucia in an institution, and would not commit her permanently to the English hospital where she was staying. Nora appears to have washed her hands of the young woman; she was worn out by the chaos that accompanied her daughter wherever she went. Since there was nowhere for Lucia to stay, Maria Jolas generously offered to bring her back to her house in Paris. But the patient was beyond any amateur help, and within three weeks Joyce's daughter had to be removed to an asylum in a straightjacket. In April 1935 Lucia was committed by her parents to the care of Dr Achille Delmas, whose private clinic at Ivry was situated a short distance outside of Paris. She would remain a residential patient in mental hospitals for the rest of her life.

Joyce never abandoned the belief that his daughter might one day recover, but it was a vain hope. Lucia's schizophrenia was a permanent and crushing condition, and he would never fully come to terms with witnessing the gradual collapse of her psyche. Nonetheless his day-to-day life went on. The Irishman's spirit, no matter how near to breaking, would endure until he had finished his last great literary experiment. Out of the darkness of his ruined sight he would make his legacy a song to the great river of life, in which human pain and human joy mingle in the flow of time and history.

CHAPTER X

THE FINAL YEARS

'The Mime of Mick Nick and the Maggies' ended with the prayer 'Lord, heap miseries upon us yet entwine our arts with laughter low.' It was a neat reflection of Joyce's state of mind as he grappled with the last chapters of *Finnegans Wake*. Lucia's illness placed a strain on both his energy and his bank balance, eating up much of his income. Most of the profits from the American edition of *Ulysses* went on paying for her medical bills, and Joyce began to draw heavily on his capital from Harriet Weaver. He and Nora lived as extravagantly as ever, taking long holidays in luxurious hotels and spending their money like water. Joyce ignored the warnings of his solicitors that his fortune was becoming dangerously depleted. 'I will go on selling,' he told Paul Leon, 'It's not my fault that the stock has fallen in price. When it is exhausted I will give lessons.'

Joyce's escape from his problems was to drink more, leading to arguments with Nora. She would not put up with his drunkenness, and left on several occasions. The separations were usually only for a day or so, since Leon or one of Joyce's other friends would persuade Nora to return home. Nonetheless the couple's recurring quarrels reflected the strain on both of them. Their precarious harmony had already been upset by their differing views on how to deal with Lucia's schizophrenia. Nora's attitude to her daughter was more practical than her husband's, and she resented his constant pandering to her every whim. Joyce's obsessive crusade to 'save' Lucia had placed great strain upon his wife, since she bore the brunt of the young woman's hysterical outbursts and madcap exploits. At her lowest moments Nora rekindled her old plan of returning to live in Galway for good, leaving her maddening husband behind, but it was just a pipe dream. They were bound together by shared decades of laughter and pain, and no amount of bickering could change that fact.

Giorgio and Helen Joyce were experiencing problems of their own in the United States, where his singing career had not taken off. In the summer of 1935 the couple returned to Paris. The ostensible reason was that Giorgio had developed a throat problem and needed an operation, but they had been warned that Joyce's health was in serious decline, and wished to be at hand in case he grew worse. In January 1938 Giorgio and Helen returned to New York because one of her close relatives was seriously ill. Joyce had grown fond of his American daughter-in-law, and was stricken by her and Giorgio's departure overseas with his grandson. He had no intention of ever visiting the United States himself, and anxiously asked the couple when they might be coming back to France. The day before they left Joyce had another shock, when Samuel Beckett was attacked and stabbed by a pimp on a Paris street. His protégé was now restored to his inner circle after the falling out over Lucia, and Joyce paid for him to be moved to a private hospital room.

Although he was embroiled in preparing *Finnegans Wake* for publication, even a man as apolitical as Joyce could not ignore the rise of Hitler or the darkness that was creeping over Europe. He retained his lifelong affinity with Jews, and loathed anti-Semitism – describing it as 'one of the easiest and oldest prejudices "to prove" '. The plight of the Jews of Germany and Austria, now facing persecution, moved him to use his influence to assist the flight of several endangered Jewish friends and intellectuals from the Nazis. In this cause he enlisted the help of his contacts in Europe and the United States, persuading them to exert pressure on the immigration authorities in their countries to grant entry visas to the refugees.

The last 'Work in Progress' episode, 'Storiella, as She is Syung', had been published in London in 1937, and the book was nearly finished. Joyce originally hoped to have it published on 2 May 1938, his late father's birthday, but the work dragged on and the date had to be put back. He had still not revealed its real title, which remained the object of much speculation. Joyce had not told even his closest friends, and jokingly offered a thousand-franc reward to the person who could guess it. In August 1938 he repeated the offer to Eugene and Maria Jolas over dinner. Nora, who had known the title for years, jokingly began singing the song 'Finnegans Wake', although she changed the protagonist's name, and called him Shannigan and Flannigan. On the next morning Eugene Jolas realized what the title must be. 'You've taken something out of me.' Joyce commented when Jolas came to him, and made his friend promise not to tell anyone. But he was also amused, and paid the debt with a huge bag of 10 franc pieces, which he delivered personally to the Jolas's flat. Perhaps, in his superstitious fashion, Joyce saw the revelation of his book's title as a good omen that his labour on it was nearly at an end.

167

Finnegans Wake was completed and sent off to its English publishers in November 1938. A proof copy was returned to him by the end of January 1939. On Joyce's birthday a few days later, his daughter-in-law Helen ordered a cake in the shape of a bookcase holding his seven published works, beginning with *Chamber Music* and ending with *Finnegans Wake*. The family and their friends ate dinner from a round mirror with models representing Paris and Dublin, the twin pillars of Joyce's life, on opposite sides. Nora wore a new ring with a bluish-green aquamarine gem, the gift of her husband, to symbolize the river that was at the centre of the new book. She was responsible for the party's most unforgettable moment, when she turned round and said 'Well, Jim, I haven't read any of your books but I'll have to some day because they must be good considering how well they sell.' Nobody will ever know for sure whether or not she was joking.

Just over three months later, in May 1939, *Finnegans Wake* was published in England by Faber & Faber, and in the United States by the Viking Press. Joyce's avalanche of words and images confused most reviewers. Oliver St John Gogarty denigrated it as a 'colossal leg pull', whilst simultaneously praising Joyce's indomitable spirit. Other critics, for example Edmund Wilson and Harry Levin, showed greater insight into his intentions, but maybe Joyce himself was the only person who could fully understand the book he had written. Nonetheless there was a beautiful and wilful poetry in the work that could not be ignored, a passion to match the broad humour that emerged from its puns, jumbled phrases and unfamiliar words. Joyce, working for long hours, and often dosed with cocaine to dull the pain in his eyes, had created a narrative that existed on a wide range of levels. Nonetheless, its ever-shifting fabric was intended to move to an underlying aesthetic purpose. The question, and it can never be resolved since it is a matter of opinion, is whether Joyce was so profligate with his obscure and labyrinthine language that he truly did write 'as a lunatic for lunatics', the accusation of the critic Desmond McCarthy. Joyce himself was ambivalent about the complexity of the book. On one hand he described it as so simple that anybody could understand it. On the other he admitted wanting to keep the critics busy for the next 300 years.

The novel's greatest character, or on another plane, natural force, is Anna Livia Plurabelle, wife of the publican Humphrey Chimpden Earwicker (HCE or Here Comes Everybody), the mother of Joyce's universal family. She is first encountered in a conversation between two washerwomen gossiping across the River Liffey at Chapelizod. Joyce recorded the last pages of the chapter, which he described as 'an attempt to subordinate words to the rhythm of water', for the BBC in 1931, after Faber & Faber published the episode separately as part of 'Work in Progress'. The washerwomen discuss the sordid details of the lives of Earwicker and his wife as they wash their underwear in the waters of the Liffey. But Anna Livia is also the spirit of the river, and *Finnegans Wake* concludes with a beautiful, almost hymn-like monologue, in which the river, or the musings of the dreaming woman, or the thoughts of the dying giant (perhaps identifiable in the author's mind with John Joyce) merge into the sea at Dublin Bay beneath the Hill of Howth, in folklore the head of Finn MacCumhall. The book, as Joyce intended from its inception, is cyclical, and ends where it began. 'The keys to. Given! A way. A lone. A last. A last. A loved. A long the ...', the line with which *Finnegans Wake* ends, is the beginning of its incomplete first sentence: 'riverrun, past Eve and Adam's, from swerve of shore to bend of bay, brings us by a commodious vicus of recirculation back to Howth Castle and Environs.'

Anna Livia, like Molly Bloom, used phrases that might have come from Nora, and shared the Galway woman's even temperament, bantering humour and disdain for the vices of her husband. It was appropriate that at the end of his last work Joyce should sing of her, the one constant in his life. For all their rows and tumults through the years, they had kept faith with the promises made to each other in 1904. They understood each other, or as much at least as a husband and wife ever can. But Joyce was worn out now, almost crippled by diminished sight and recurring stomach illness. To add to his woes the marriage of his son was in difficulties. In the last months of 1938 Helen suffered a nervous breakdown, and was hospitalized. Joyce, who was worried for her, sent flowers and suggested she 'Cheer up for the love of Giorgio', but an unbridgeable chasm had opened up between the husband and wife. After her release Helen recovered temporarily, but her mental health soon deteriorated and Giorgio turned against her.

Within a few months Joyce's personal troubles were overshadowed by the declaration of the Second World War. His first concern was for his daughter. Dr Delmas had made contingency plans to evacuate the inmates to a hotel in La Baule, some distance from the French capital, but when Joyce and Nora went to the town in late August 1939 to await their daughter's arrival, they were horrified to discover that the arrangements had broken down. It was mid-September before the doctor could find alternative accommodation in the adjacent town of Pornichet, and move his patients out of Paris. Lucia was terrified that the Germans were going to bomb the hospital, and her father was unwilling to leave until she had calmed down. They were still in La Baule when Giorgio rang to tell them that he had left his wife, and was now taking Stephen from her because she was incapable of looking after the child. At the end of October the Irishman and Nora returned to Paris to help their son in his crisis. Joyce did not know that he would never see his daughter Lucia again.

The break-up of Giorgio's marriage led to a temporary estrangement between Joyce and his most trusted adviser. Paul Leon was a close friend of Helen Kastor Fleischman, and reckoned that her illness was no more than hysteria caused by her husband's rejection. Giorgio wanted Helen to be sent back to the United States for treatment, and asked Leon to approach her brother Robert Kastor on his behalf. Joyce was furious with Leon for refusing his son's request, and demanded the return of all the publishers' contracts he was keeping. Leon was deeply hurt, and the two men were estranged for several months. The quarrel was not healed until the invasion of France in April 1940, when the Joyces and Paul Leon met as refugees in La Chapelle. Leon, fleeing from the approaching Germans, turned up at the building where Joyce was sheltering with Nora, and the two old friends were quickly reconciled.

During the months following the declaration of the war, Joyce fretted over Lucia and his grandson, both of whom had been sent away from Paris. Stephen was now boarding in the country at Maria Jolas's school in Saint Gerand le Puy, but Joyce believed he was lonely and missing his parents. Giorgio was temporarily avoiding his parents after the acrimony of his separation, whilst Helen had become so ill the authorities had placed her in a mental hospital for her own safety. The sundering apart of Joyce's family was paralleled by the changes that war had brought to Paris. The free and easy café society of the 1920s and 30s was breaking up, as war shortages began to bite; and expatriate intellectuals, many of them Jewish, left the city. Joyce felt depressed and exhausted, and he and Nora were finding Paris unbearable. His reaction to the stress he felt was to drink more heavily, and to waste his money on unnecessary luxuries. 'We are going downhill fast', he told Beckett, and it was clear that he was on the verge of a breakdown himself.

In December 1939 Joyce and Nora abandoned Paris, their home for nearly twenty years, to go and stay at a hotel in Saint Gerand. They left most of their possessions behind, intending to return when the situation improved, but it was the Irishman's farewell to the city that had witnessed his greatest literary triumphs. He would never return to the French capital. The family, now only James, Nora, Giorgio and Stephen, spent Christmas Day with Maria Jolas, whose husband was in the United States. Joyce was excessively melancholy at first, but later cheered up and ended the evening dancing with his hostess. Joyce and Nora stayed on in the small town after the holidays, although there was little for him to do except make a few corrections for the next edition of *Finnegans Wake*. After the book's tepid reception he lacked the enthusiasm or energy to begin anything new. Although Beckett came to visit him, Joyce was lonely away from the social and cultural buzz of Paris. He was suffering badly from stomach pains, although he refused to see a doctor, fearing he might be told he had stomach cancer. For several months he and Nora lingered on in the quiet provincial town. Joyce made friends with the local people, and fought his own small war with the dogs that swarmed on its narrow streets.

In June 1940 the Germans launched the great offensive that broke open the French lines and brought their armies to the gates of Paris. Joyce had temporarily moved to Vichy at the time, but he returned to Saint Gerand, where Giorgio, Beckett and Paul Leon soon arrived from the threatened capital. After the French defeat, the Germans occupied Paris and the north of the country, leaving the south under the control of the puppet Vichy government. Leon and Beckett opted to return to Paris when some semblance of normality had been restored, but it was obvious the Joyces, including Giorgio and Stephen, would have to leave France. Maria Jolas had returned to the United States, and wrote urging Joyce to go there, but he had no desire to flee to a country that he professed to dislike. Instead he decided to go to neutral Switzerland, his haven during the First World War. One of the major factors in this choice was the plight of Lucia, who was still at Ivry. It was not easy for the Joyces to obtain permission to enter Switzerland, in part because the immigration authorities did not realize who he was at first. Eventually the Mayor of Zurich intervened to offer the famous refugee sanctuary, but the slowness of the negotiations put the family at risk of internment. When their visas were at last granted they were forced to leave Lucia in France, intending her to follow them to Zurich once they were settled there. Joyce and Nora's sadness was increased by the news of the death of Mrs Barnacle in Galway. He was reduced to tears by this reminder of his own mortality.

The Joyces arrived in Zurich on the evening of 18 December 1940 and installed themselves in two rooms at the Hotel Pension Delphin. There was little for Joyce to do except fill the empty hours, and he spent his days out walking with his grandson Stephen. He socialized little although he was happy to meet any old acquaintances from the Zurich years. Siegfried Giedion, a Swiss art critic who had known the Joyces in Paris, invited them to spend Christmas Day at his home. After the meal Joyce and Giorgio entertained the guests by singing duets in Irish and Latin, a pleasant echo of the Yuletides of the author's Dublin childhood. The first days of 1941 brought a letter from Stanislaus, who had been forced to leave his home in Trieste by the Italian authorities and was in Florence. Joyce wrote his brother a postcard with the names of some people who might help him in his predicament.

It was an irony that the last written words of the greatest literary genius of the century were to the brother who had been beside him at the beginning of his illustrious career. Two days later Joyce dined with Nora at the Kronenhalle, one of his favourite restaurants in Zurich. After they returned home Joyce was stricken with stomach pains. He was admitted to hospital on the next day, and diagnosed as having a burst duodenal ulcer. At first he refused the operation he desperately needed, and it was only after Giorgio reassured him it wasn't cancer that he gave his permission. The operation was carried out on the morning of Saturday 9 January, and appeared to have saved his life. When Joyce came out from the anesthetic he told Nora: 'I thought I wouldn't get through it', and seemed in good spirits. But on the following morning he began to fail from peritonitis, and slipped into a coma. He revived to ask that Nora's bed be placed beside his, and later woke again to request that she and Giorgio be sent for. At two o'clock, on the morning of 13 January 1941 a doctor rang Nora and summoned her to the hospital, but it was too late. Before she and Giorgio could arrive James Joyce, writer, husband and exile, died alone on his hospital bed.

Joyce's funeral, at the Fluntern cemetery near the Zurich zoo, was modest enough considering his worldwide reputation. There were no flowers, since Joyce disliked them, and Nora insisted no religious service take place. 'I couldn't do that to him,' she informed a priest who offered to officiate. Following three short speeches a tenor sang Monteverdi's 'Addio terra, addio cielo,' and the writer's simple wooden coffin was lowered into the ground. Lucia, far away in the asylum at Ivry, would not believe that her eminent father was dead. 'What is he doing under the ground, that idiot?' she said to Nino Frank. 'When will he decide to come out? He's watching us all the time.'

No writer as important as Joyce could be ignored forever, but in the turmoil of the Second World War his passing was a brief footnote. Harriet Weaver heard of it on the radio a few hours later, and immediately sent some money to Nora. During the coming years, as Joyce's widow untangled the confused web of Joyce's finances, the Englishwoman provided the same support she once gave the dead writer. After Nora's death she was appointed Lucia's guardian, and had her charge transferred to a hospital in Northampton where she could visit her. As Joyce's literary executor Harriet Weaver tried to persuade Nora to let her donate the manuscripts of 'Exiles' and *Finnegans Wake* to the National Library of Ireland, but the widow was too bitter to let them go to his native city.

Harriet Weaver, the patroness and friend of James Joyce, died in 1961.

Nora, to the surprise of many of her friends, opted to stay in Zurich, close to the body of her husband. There she lived quietly until her death in 1951. At times she came close to abject poverty, and was nearly reduced to selling her most precious memento of her husband, a signed copy of *Chamber Music*. Fortunately she was spared that ignominy, and spent her last few years in reasonable comfort. Nora never forgave Ireland for its neglect of James Joyce. In 1948 the Irish government brought the body of W. B. Yeats, Ireland's greatest poet, back from France to Sligo for burial with official honours, but the body of the country's greatest novelist was left in its Swiss exile. Perhaps Joyce's spirit was happy to remain in Zurich. 'I often think he must like the cemetery he is in,' Nora informed one journalist before her death. 'It is near the zoo and you can hear the lions roar'. After her death in 1951 she too was buried in the Fluntern Cemetery, but there was no room to place her grave beside her husband's, and Nora's body had to be interred some distance away from his. Giorgio remained in Zurich with his mother after Joyce's death, and was re-married to a Swiss eye-specialist in 1954. In 1946 his son Stephen left Switzerland to be educated in the United States, where his mother Helen, who had recovered from her nervous breakdown, was now living. Giorgio Joyce died in 1976, and was buried near to his parents. His sister Lucia lingered on in Northampton until 1982. She chose to be buried near the hospital where she had spent the last thirty years of her life, rather than in Zurich with the rest of her family.

Paul Leon remained too long in Paris sorting out his affairs, and was arrested by the German; he died in an internment camp near the city in 1942. Samuel Beckett, who returned to Paris at the same time, joined the Resistance and survived. He took on Joyce's mantle of the exiled writer and achieved world fame with his play 'Waiting for Godot'. Before his death in 1989 Beckett became the third Irishman to receive the Nobel Prize for Literature, an accolade never granted to the great Irish writer who was his early guide and inspiration. Stanislaus Joyce returned to Trieste after the Second World War. He died in 1955, leaving behind a huge cache of his brother's correspondence, including the 'dirty letters' to Nora. In 1957 Stanislaus's widow sold the entire collection to Cornell University for almost $50,000. His own recollections of his famous brother may be found in two posthumous volumes – *My Brother's Keeper* (1958) and *Stanislaus Joyce's Dublin Diary* (1962).

The collection of Joyce papers in Cornell University is just one of dozens scattered through America and the British Isles. The Irishman was a prodigious hoarder of his own writings and notes, whilst his extant letters range from the long correspondence with Harriet Weaver (in the British Library) to four love letters written to Marthe Fleischmann in 1919. All these archives help fuel what might be called the 'Joyce industry' – the extraordinary torrent of academic and popular books that dissect every possible aspect of his work. No writer has ever been as amenable to this kind of analysis as Joyce – the vast range and complexity of his literary output can be interpreted to suit every scholarly taste and fad. Yet even though Joyce wrote as a Jesuit for other Jesuits, his primary desire, like any other good novelist, was to divert, move and amuse his readers. One suspects that he was never quite as serious about his writings as some of the Joyce scholars who devote years of their lives to unravelling his every word.

Joyce's reputation in Ireland since his death has been transformed from what might be called 'official leper' to national hero. In fact there always was a far greater sympathy for his writings in his homeland than was publicly acknowledged. Joyce's genius was as essentially Irish as the Dublin landscape of his books, and his influence saturated the writing of several generations of Irish writers. From the 1950s onwards Ireland slowly began to embrace him as its greatest literary figure of the century. In 1954 a small group of enthusiasts, including the poet Patrick Kavanagh, participated in the first 'Bloomsday' celebration of *Ulysses*. As the hundredth anniversary of that June day in 1904 comes closer, the life and works of James Joyce have become part of the cultural fabric of his native country.

CHRONOLOGY

1882   Birth of James Joyce in Rathgar, Dublin (2 February), the eldest surviving son of John Joyce and Mary Joyce (nee Murray).

1884   Birth of Stanislaus Joyce. Nora Barnacle born in Galway.

1887   The Joyce family moves to Martello Terrace, Bray.

1888   Joyce is enrolled at the Jesuit school Clongowes Wood in County Kildare.

1891   Joyce writes the poem 'Et Tu Healy' following the death of C. S. Parnell. He is forced to leave Clongowes Wood School because of his father's financial problems.

1893   James and Stanislaus Joyce enter Belvedere College as non fee-paying students.

1894   Joyce accompanies his father John Joyce to Cork for the sale of his remaining properties in the county.

1896   Joyce loses his virginity to a Dublin prostitute. Later in the year he has a profound religious experience at a Retreat run by the noted Jesuit preacher Father Cullen.

1897   Joyce loses his religious faith.

1898   Joyce leaves Belvedere and enters University College
        Dublin, where he studies modern languages.

1900   Joyce gives a lecture on Ibsen at the UCD Literary
        and Historical Society. Later in the year he publishes
        an article on Ibsen's 'When We Dead Awaken' in the
        Fortnightly Review. He writes a play (now lost) called
        'A Brilliant Career'.

1901   Joyce publishes 'Day of the Rabblement', an attack on
        the Irish Literary Revival.

1902   Joyce's youngest brother George dies at age fifteen of
        peritonitis. Joyce meets W. B. Yeats and shows him his
        poems and epiphanies. In December he goes to Paris,
        intending to continue his medical training. Joyce writes
        his first reviews for *Daily Express*.

1903   Meeting with John Millington Synge in Paris. Mary
        Joyce dies of cancer.

1904   Joyce begins writing *Stephen Hero*. He meets Nora
        Barnacle on Nassau Street (10 June) and begins an
        affair with her (16 June). Joyce writes 'The Sisters'
        and two other stories for the *Irish Homestead*, and
        plans *Dubliners*. He begins singing in public. Pri-
        vately publishes 'The Holy Office', an attack on Irish
        writers, after it is rejected by *St Stephen's* magazine.
        In October Joyce and Nora Barnacle elope to Eu-

rope. They settle in Pola, in Austrian–held Italy, where Joyce takes up a teaching position at the Berlitz School.

1905   Joyce and Nora move to Trieste, where he works as a language teacher. Stanislaus joins them there. *Dubliners* is submitted to Grant Richards for publication. Birth of Giorgio Joyce.

1906   Joyce completes *Stephen Hero*. He moves to Rome to take up a banking position. Grant Richards rejects *Dubliners*.

1907   Joyce leaves bank and returns to Trieste. *Chamber Music* published. He writes the short story 'The Dead' and begins to turn *Stephen Hero* into *A Portrait of the Artist as a Young Man*. Birth of Lucia Joyce.

1909   Joyce visits Ireland with Giorgio, where he visits Nora's family in Galway, then has a breakdown after Vincent Cosgrave claims to have seduced Nora in 1904. Returns later in the year to open the 'Volta', Ireland's first cinema. Period of the 'dirty letters' correspondence with Nora.

1910   Joyce returns to Trieste with his sister Eveline.

1912   Nora and the children accompany Joyce on his final visit to Ireland. He writes 'She Weeps above Rahoon' after a visit to the grave of Michael Furey in Galway. Joyce leaves Ireland in a rage after his printers destroy the sheets of *Dubliners*. Writes the satirical poem 'Gas from a Burner' on his way back to Trieste.

1913   Ezra Pound contacts Joyce at the suggestion of W. B. Yeats, and helps him find publishers for his works.

1914   The *Egoist* begins publishing *A Portrait of the Artist as a Young Man* as a serial. Joyce writes the play 'Exiles' and begins *Ulysses*. *Dubliners* published by Grant Richards. World War I begins.

1915   Stanislaus Joyce interned in Trieste for his pro-Italian political views. Joyce and his family leave Trieste and move to Zurich.

1916   *A Portrait of the Artist as a Young Man* published by B. W. Huebsch.

1917   Harriet Weaver begins giving Joyce money anonymously. Joyce has the first of many operations on his eyes.

1918   The *Little Review* magazine begins serializing *Ulysses* in the United States. Joyce co-manages the 'Irish Players' theatre company in Zurich. Nora takes a role in their production of J. M. Synge's *Riders to the Sea*.

1919   Joyce returns to Trieste with his family.

1920   Joyce moves to Paris on the advice of Ezra Pound. The publishers of the *Little Review* are fined, and *Ulysses* banned in the United States, after a complaint from the New York Society for the Prevention of Vice.

1921　Sylvia Beach of Shakespeare and Company agrees to publish *Ulysses,* after B. W. Huebsch declines the novel.

1922　*Ulysses* published on 2 February, Joyce's fortieth birthday. Nora and the children return to Dublin and Galway, but flee back to Paris after coming under crossfire between the opposing factions in the Irish Civil War.

1923　Joyce begins *Finnegans Wake,* but does not reveal the book's title.

1924　First excerpts from *Finnegans Wake* published as 'Work in Progress' in *Transatlantic Review.*

1925　More extracts of 'Work in Progress' published.

1926　*Two Worlds Monthly* begins its pirated serialization of *Ulysses.*

1927　The 'International Protest' against the pirating of *Ulysses* is published. *Transition* magazine, edited by Eugene Jolas, publishes the first of seventeen instalments of 'Work in Progress'.

1928　'Anna Livia Plurabelle' published in New York.

1929　'Tales told of Shem and Shaun' published by the Black

Sun Press. 'Our Exagimation round his Factification for Incamination of his Work in Progress' published by Shakespeare and Company. *Ulysse*, the French translation of *Ulysses* published; the event is celebrated at the 'Déjeuner *Ulysse*', arranged by Sylvia Beach and Adrienne Monnier.

1930   Joyce undergoes the first of a series of eye operations carried out by Dr Albert Vogt in Zurich. Samuel Beckett is barred from the Joyce household after Nora complains he has been trifling with Lucia's affections. Giorgio Joyce marries Helen Kastor Fleischman. Joyce begins promoting the Irish tenor John Sullivan.

1931   Joyce and Nora are married at Kensington Registry Office, London. Sylvia Beach returns the publishing rights to *Ulysses*. John Joyce dies in Dublin (29 December).

1932   Birth of Joyce's grandson Stephen, son of Giorgio and Helen; shortly afterwards Joyce writes the poem 'Ecce Puer'. Paul Leon becomes Joyce's unpaid secretary and literary agent. After several years of psychological disturbances, Lucia Joyce develops schizophrenia.

1933   The ban on *Ulysses* in the United States is lifted after Judge John M. Woolsey rules that it is not obscene. Odyssey Press (Hamburg) publishes a European edition.

1934   The first American edition of *Ulysses* is published by

Random House. Giorgio and Helen Joyce leave for the United States. 'The Mime of Mick Nick and the Maggies' is published.

1935   Lucia Joyce is committed to the care of Dr Delmas at Ivry.

1936   *Collected Poems* published in New York. *Ulysses* published in London by John Lane.

1937   'Storiella as she is Syung', the last 'Work in Progress' instalment, is published.

1938   'Work in Progress' finished. Eugene Jolas guesses the book's title will be *Finnegans Wake* and wins 1,000 francs from Joyce.

1939   *Finnegans Wake* is published by Faber & Faber in England, and the Viking Press in the United States. The Second World War begins. Giorgio Joyce separates from his wife. Joyce visits his daughter Lucia for the last time. He and Nora Joyce leave Paris for St Gerand le-Puy (December).

1940   The Germans conquer France and occupy Paris. Joyce, Nora, Giorgio and Stephen flee to Zurich, Switzerland.

1941   James Joyce dies of peritonitis following a burst duodenal ulcer in Zurich (13 January). He is buried at the Fluntern cemetery.

1942 Paul Leon, Joyce's friend and secretary, dies in a Nazi internment camp.

1944 *Stephen Hero* is published posthumously.

1951 Nora Joyce dies in Zurich. Harriet Weaver becomes Lucia Joyce's guardian and transfers her from Ivry to St Andrews Hospital in Northampton, where she spends the rest of her life.

1954 The first 'Bloomsday' is celebrated in Dublin.

1955 Death of Stanislaus Joyce.

1959 Richard Ellman's classic biography *James Joyce* is published.

1961 Death of Harriet Shaw Weaver.

1976 Death of Giorgio Joyce.

1982 Death of Lucia Joyce.